WORLD WAR 2
FACTS BOOK

WW2 History Book for Adults - From the Greatest Battles of WW2 to the Leaders, Military Tactics and Strategy of the War

CHARLES NILSEN

CONTENTS

INTRODUCTION

The Second World War unfolded as a global conflict, unleashing violence that gripped the entire world from London in the West to Pearl Harbor in the East. The destruction witnessed during this war seems unparalleled to this day. The conflict involved the use of atomic bombs for the first time and resulted in an estimated 70-85 million fatalities. Among these, millions perished in genocides, most notably during the Holocaust in Nazi Germany, one of the worst calamities in history that claimed the lives of over six million European Jews.

The war was fought between the Allies and the Axis powers, with the former including the United States of America, the United Kingdom, France, and the Soviet Union, and the latter comprising Germany, Italy, and Japan. This comprehensive book aims to shed light on the various nuances of war, covering important battles, details about key leaders, military strategies and weapons, resistance movements, treaties, causes, and the war's overall effects and outcomes.

In the opening chapter of this book, we delve into some of the important causes of World War 2. After the First World War ended, Germany perceived the Treaty of Versailles as a threat to its nationhood, as it had burdened Germany with substantial financial penalties disguised as war reparations imposed by Western countries. These penalties had proved detrimental to Germany, causing several economic challenges and widespread poverty, ultimately creating a fertile ground for the emergence of right-wing nationalism. Seizing this as an opportunity, Adolf Hitler of the Nazi Party effectively gathered mass support for his fascist right-wing agenda, ultimately taking power. Initially met with a policy of appeasement by Western nations, Hitler's invasion of Poland was a tipping point and was viewed as a threat by these nations. The first chapter of this book extensively explores these significant causes of the Second World War, including the profound impact of the Great Depression.

In the second chapter, we delve into some of the significant battles fought during the war. These events are presented chronologically, with detailed discussions on each. Notable engagements include the Invasion of Poland and the Winter War in 1939, the Battle of Britain and the Battle of France in 1940, Operation Barbarossa and the Pearl Harbor Incident in 1941, the Battle of Stalingrad and the Battle of Midway in 1942, the Battle of Kursk and the Invasion of Sicily in 1943, and finally, the D-Day, the Battle of Bulge, and the bombings of Hiroshima and Nagasaki in 1944-45.

Turning to the third chapter, we delve into the intricacies of some key leaders during the war. The Allies were primarily led by the Prime Minister of Britain, Winston Churchill, President Franklin D. Roosevelt of the United States, Joseph Stalin of the Soviet Union, and Chiang Kai-Shek of China. On the other side, the Axis powers were under the leadership of Adolf Hitler and his chief military strategist, Heinrich Himmler, in the case of Germany, Benito Mussolini of Italy, and Hideko Tojo and Emperor Hirohito of Japan.

Moving on to the fourth chapter, we thoroughly compare and contrast the Allies and Axis powers, examining their ideologies, strategies, strengths, and weaknesses. The Allies rooted their ideology in principles of democracy, freedom, and opposition to authoritarian regimes, exemplified by their stand against Nazi Germany and Imperial Japan. Conversely, the Axis powers' ideology centered around fascism, militarism, and expansionism. This chapter delves deeply into both sides' nuanced strengths and weaknesses, providing a comprehensive understanding of this aspect of the war.

In the succeeding fifth chapter of our book, we explore the diverse resistance movements that unfolded across different theatres of the war. While commonly termed as resistance movements in the European Theatre, the Pacific Theatre witnessed resistance in the form of guerrilla warfare.

Moving on to Chapter Six, we delve into the critical role of espionage and intelligence gathering during the war. Noteworthy espionage techniques include the contributions of code-breakers like Alan Turing and the operations of spy networks such as OSS and Abwehr. Additionally, we delve into the significant tools and techniques, such as the Enigma Machine—a cipher device extensively employed by Nazi Germany to encode secret messages, utilizing an electromechanical rotor mechanism to scramble the 26 letters of the alphabet.

Proceeding to the subsequent chapter, we emphasize the significant role played by women in the war. Often underestimated by historians, the contribution of women during the conflict was substantial. They not only undertook economic roles by taking up jobs left by male counterparts but also served as nurses and medical staff members. They also actively participated in the military service through organizations such as the WAAC.

Chapter Eight scrutinizes the military tactics, technology and weaponry employed by the Axis and the Allies during the war. Nazi Germany's prominent technique, the Blitzkrieg, or lightning war, is discussed in depth. Similarly, we shed light on strategies like Island

Hopping and Guerrilla Warfare, primarily utilized by the Western Allied Powers in the Pacific Theatre against Japan. This chapter also comprehensively discusses various aerial warfare techniques, such as carpet bombing, amongst others.

Chapter Nine sheds light on propaganda as a tool employed by both the Allies and Axis powers to gather support for their war ambitions. In the case of the Axis powers, figures like Hitler and Joseph Goebbels, the Minister of Public Enlightenment and Propaganda, played significant roles. Nazi propaganda strategically targeted discrimination against ethnic Germans in Eastern European nations while vilifying the Jewish community. The chapter further explores how both the Allies and Axis powers utilized radio broadcasts, pamphlets, films, and newsreels to disseminate their propaganda messages among their citizenry.

Discussing one of the most horrifying genocides in history, Chapter Ten delves into the Holocaust. It provides an in-depth exploration of the term's origins, the so-called Nazi "final solution," concentration camps, gas chambers, crematoria, and the Nuremberg Laws of 1935.

In Chapter Eleven, we examine the far-reaching effects of the war, which impacted large segments of society. Some of the prominent themes discussed in this book range from the deaths of innocent individuals to the effects of rationing, the impacts on children's education, and the consequences of refugees and migration.

In the final chapter of our book, we will cover the final battles and the end of the war.

Overall, this book serves as a concise overview of the Second World War, touching upon a wide range of aspects, including a comparison of strengths and weaknesses of the two sides, military tactics and strategies, different events, and the profound impacts of the war.

1

CAUSES OF THE WAR

I n this first chapter of our book, we begin our exploration into the tumultuous period of the Second World War by delving into the complex web of events and circumstances that set the stage for one of the most disastrous conflicts in human history. It is estimated that the conflict took the lives of 70-85 million people, or about 3% of the world population at the time. In this chapter, we delve into factors that contributed to the outbreak of World War 2. At its heart lies the Treaty of Versailles, a document that not only marked the end of the First World War but also sowed the seeds of discontent and resentment in Germany. The punitive measures imposed on Germany, coupled with the failure of international institutions like the League of Nations, set the stage for the rise of hypernationalism and the ascension of Adolf Hitler and his authoritative Nazi Party. As we navigate through the political landscape of the time, we also explore the expansionist policies of not only Germany but also Japan and Italy, shedding light on the geopolitical dynamics that paved the way for global conflict. The chapter concludes by examining the impact of the Great Depression, an economic cataclysm that further strained international relations and provided fertile ground for the rise of authoritarian regimes such as Hitler's.

The Treaty of Versailles

World War 2, marked by widespread devastation, was a tragic conflict that engulfed vast regions across the globe, spanning from the United Kingdom to Japan. The war lasted for six years, from 1939 to 1945. After all, what led to the outbreak of another global conflict just two decades after the First World War ended? The reasons are multifaceted and wide-ranging.

In the aftermath of the war, the Treaty of Versailles emerged as an important peace agreement signed by the belligerent parties. This treaty marked the cessation of hostilities between Germany and the Allied Powers. However, remarkably, Germany was not a participant in the negotiation process but was rather coerced into signing the treaty.

One of the most significant and contentious clauses in the treaty attributed full blame to Germany, stating, "The Allied and Associated Governments affirm, and Germany accepts, the responsibility of Germany and her allies for causing all the loss and damage suffered by the Allied and Associated Governments and their nationals because of the war imposed upon them by the aggression of Germany and her allies."

Therefore, Germany was compelled to disarm and bear the burden of hefty reparations to specific countries within the Allied Powers. These reparations amounted to an exorbitant sum, equivalent to nearly $442 billion in today's currency. This punitive treatment left Germany not only economically drained but also deeply humiliated. Article 231 of the treaty, often referred to as the 'war guilt clause,' placed full responsibility for the outbreak of World War 1 squarely on Germany. This not only fuelled a sense of humiliation but also led many Germans to feel unjustly scapegoated for the war, fostering feelings of victimhood and resentment. Moreover, in addition to the financial reparations, the treaty resulted in substantial territorial losses for Germany, seen by many as a violation of the principle of self-determination championed during the negotiations. Among these territorial losses were Alsace-Lorraine to France, Eupen-Malmedy to Belgium, and the establishment of the Free City of Danzig (now Gdańsk, Poland).

Furthermore, Germany forfeited its overseas colonies because of the treaty, symbolizing the nation's diminished global status.

Hypernationalism in Germany and the Rise of the Nazi Party

In the aftermath of the Treaty of Versailles, Germany's economy experienced a devastating downturn characterized by hyperinflation and widespread unemployment. This economic turmoil unleashed a wave of chaos and instability within the country. During such times of crisis, people often seek refuge in nationalist movements for a sense of stability and identity.

Amid the growing political radicalization, extremist nationalist and right-wing groups began to gain prominence. One notable example was the National Socialist German Workers' Party, commonly known as the Nazi Party. Exploiting nationalist grievances, this party ascended to power in the 1930s with Adolf Hitler at its helm.

Hitler in Power

When Hitler assumed leadership of Nazi Germany, he played an essential role in triggering World War 2 through a series of aggressive actions, expansionist policies, and violations of international agreements. One of his initial actions was the rapid expansion and modernization of the German military, which clearly defied the Treaty of Versailles that had imposed stringent limits on Germany's armed forces. While his militarization efforts raised alarm among other European powers, they initially responded with appeasement.

Hitler's Aggression and Territorial Expansion

One of Hitler's initial significant acts of aggression occurred in 1936 with the remilitarization of the Rhineland. This action clearly violated the Treaty of Versailles and the Locarno Treaties, both of which had guaranteed the demilitarization of this region. Despite this breach, Western democracies, especially France and Britain, refrained from taking any substantial measures to halt Hitler's actions.

Similarly, Hitler orchestrated the annexation of Austria into Nazi Germany, a maneuver referred to as the Anschluss. This move constituted yet another violation of international agreements and treaties and underscored Hitler's expansionist ambitions. Nonetheless, the international community again failed to mount a significant response.

Munich Agreement (1938)

When Hitler aimed to annex Sudetenland, an ethnically German region of Czechoslovakia, the Munich Agreement granted him permission to do so. In exchange, he pledged not to pursue any additional territorial expansion. However, this policy of appeasement proved ineffective in restraining Hitler, as he persisted in his aggressive expansionist agenda. In less than a year following the agreement, Hitler breached it by occupying the remaining portions of Czechoslovakia.

Nazi-Soviet Pact

One of Hitler's most significant diplomatic moves before the outbreak of World War 2 occurred in August 1939 with the signing of the Molotov-Ribbentrop Pact alongside the Soviet Union. This non-aggression pact contained a secret protocol that effectively divided Eastern Europe into spheres of influence, granting Hitler the freedom to invade Poland without concern for Soviet intervention. Emboldened by this pact, Hitler ordered the invasion of Poland on September 1, 1939, a clear act of aggression and a direct violation of international law.

In response to this invasion, Britain and France fulfilled their commitments to Poland and declared war on Germany on September 3, 1939, officially marking the commencement of World War 2.

Expansionist Policies of Japan and Italy

Like Germany, Japan and Italy pursued expansionist policies in the years leading up to World War 2, which contributed to the outbreak of the war. Some of these have been outlined hereunder:

Japanese Invasion of Manchuria (1931): Despite the considerable odds, Japan's ambitions in Asia manifested prominently through the 1931 invasion of Manchuria. This incursion not only infringed upon China's sovereignty but also resulted in the establishment of the puppet state of Manchukuo. While the international community denounced Japan's actions, no substantial interventions were taken to thwart them.

Japanese Invasion of China (Second Sino-Japanese War, 1937): The comprehensive invasion of China in 1937 marked a significant intensification of Japan's expansionist policies. This conflict, recognized as the Second Sino-Japanese War, resulted in widespread atrocities and a brutal occupation.

Japanese Withdrawal from the League of Nations (1933): In 1933, Japan's withdrawal from the League of Nations followed international criticism of its actions in Manchuria. This decision represented a shift away from international diplomacy and clearly indicated Japan's decision to pursue its expansionist objectives independently.

Tripartite Pact (1940): In September 1940, Japan joined the Axis Powers by signing the Tripartite Pact with Germany and Italy. This pact formalized their alliance and committed Japan to support Axis military efforts.

Italian Conquest of Ethiopia (1935-1936): Italy also followed a policy of expansionism. Under the leadership of Benito Mussolini, it invaded Ethiopia in 1935. This act of aggression violated international agreements and the principles of collective security. Despite sanctions imposed by the League of Nations, Italy successfully annexed Ethiopia.

Spanish Civil War (1936-1939): Italy and Germany supported General Francisco Franco's Nationalist forces during the Spanish Civil War (1936-1939). This involvement in a foreign civil conflict allowed Italy to gain influence in Spain and further demonstrated its expansionist ambitions.

Italian invasion of Albania (1939): Italy invaded Albania in April 1939, adding to Mussolini's expanding colonial empire. While Albania was a relatively small conquest, it demonstrated Italy's willingness to pursue territorial expansion in the Balkans.

The failure of League of Nations

As mentioned, the League of Nations was established after World War I to promote international cooperation, prevent conflicts, and ensure enduring peace. However, it grappled with several critical shortcomings that ultimately hindered its ability to forestall the outbreak of another global conflict.

One of its primary failures lay in its inability to effectively address major international crises, exemplified by its incapacity to halt the Japanese invasion of Manchuria in 1931. Furthermore, the League faced limitations in its membership and influence (Eloranta, 2010). Notably, the United States, despite advocating for the League's formation, never became a member, diminishing its global reach. Additionally, significant powers such as Germany and the Soviet Union were absent from its membership for extended periods, limiting the League's capacity to mediate disputes. Its effectiveness in enforcing decisions relied on member states supplying troops and resources, a process often sluggish and hesitant due to the absence of its dedicated military force.

Another vital factor in its downfall was the trend of nations, especially during the early years of the Great Depression, turning inward and adopting economic isolationist policies (Moser, 2015). This trend eroded international economic cooperation and contributed to the collapse of the global economic order. Lastly, there were issues inherent in the League of Nations' approach to international conflicts, which leaned toward reactivity rather than proactivity. The League frequently focused on addressing the immediate symptoms of conflicts rather than delving into their root causes, such as economic turmoil, political instability, and nationalist grievances, which fuelled aggression in Europe and Asia.

The Great Depression

The economic downturn of 1929, commonly known as the Great Depression, also played a significant role in the lead-up to World War 2 by creating conditions conducive to the outbreak of the war. The widespread economic hardships during the Great Depression triggered social and political unrest in numerous countries. In the absence of effective solutions to their economic woes, extremist movements gained traction, which included the ascent of Hitler in Germany.

Broadly speaking, many countries responded to the economic crisis by adopting nationalist and protectionist policies. Measures such as imposing high tariffs and erecting trade barriers were designed to safeguard domestic industries and jobs. However, they inadvertently led to reduced international trade and cooperation. This wave of economic nationalism contributed to diplomatic relations breaking down and heightened economic tensions between nations.

As countries became increasingly preoccupied with their own economic challenges and less inclined to collaborate with others, the Great Depression strained international relations. Nations in debt, like Germany, were grappled with making reparations payments, which led to tensions with creditor nations such as France and the United Kingdom. Furthermore, the economic depression eroded confidence in democratic governments and institutions. In certain countries, such economic conditions fuelled the emergence of authoritarian regimes that promised stability and economic recovery. These regimes would later become integral members of the Axis, i.e., Germany, Italy, and Japan.

2

MAJOR BATTLES OF WORLD WAR 2

I n this chapter, we seek to offer insights into a list of key battles fought during the Second World War, presenting them chronologically. The exploration begins with Hitler's forces invading Poland in 1939, progresses through the pivotal event of Pearl Harbor in 1941, and culminates in the profound impact of the Atomic Bombings on Hiroshima and Nagasaki in 1945. By delving into these, we aim to provide a comprehensive understanding of the significant turning points that shaped the course of the war. The Battle of Berlin will be covered in the last chapter, Chapter 12, titled "End of the War".

Invasion of Poland

September 1, 1939

The invasion of Poland on September 1, 1939, marked the commencement of World War 2 in Europe and bore significant historical implications. This invasion was notable for several key reasons. Firstly, it was distinguished by the deployment of Blitzkrieg, or "lightning warfare," a military strategy reliant on rapid-moving tanks, artillery, and infantry, complemented by air power. This swift and coordinated assault overwhelmed Polish defenses.

Concurrently, as Germany initiated its Western invasion, the Soviet Union, led by Joseph Stalin, advanced into Poland from the east on September 17, 1939. This move was in adherence to the Molotov-Ribbentrop Pact, a confidential non-aggression agreement between Nazi Germany and the Soviet Union. The invasion also featured the extensive use of overwhelming ground and air forces. In terms of ground forces, it involved approximately 1.5 million German troops, coupled with extensive air raids on Polish cities by the German Luftwaffe. Despite the resolute resistance of Polish forces, German troops managed to capture Warsaw, the Polish capital, following a brutal siege.

In the aftermath of this invasion, Britain and France responded by declaring war on Germany on September 3, 1939, honoring their commitments to Poland. This declaration officially marked the onset of World War 2. The invasion of Poland yielded profound and far-reaching consequences. It ignited World War 2 in Europe, leading to widespread destruction, suffering, and loss of life. The war persisted for six additional years, reshaping the course of history and ultimately culminating in the defeat of Nazi Germany and the end of the war in 1945.

Winter War

November 30, 1939 - March 12, 1940

The Winter War, fought between the Soviet Union and Finland from November 30, 1939, to March 12, 1940, was a brief but significant conflict with several notable facts. The war began when the Soviet Union, led by Joseph Stalin, launched a surprise invasion of Finland. The Soviet leadership claimed the need for territorial adjustments and security concerns. Disproportionate forces marked the war: the Soviet Union had a massive advantage in manpower and military equipment. The Red Army had over 1 million troops, while the Finnish forces numbered around 340,000. However, despite being outnumbered and outgunned, the Finnish forces, known for their determination and skill in winter warfare, put up a fierce resistance. They utilized guerrilla tactics and took advantage of Finland's harsh terrain and the severe winter weather to slow the Soviet advance down. As a result, the Soviet Union suffered heavy casualties during the conflict, with estimates ranging from 126,000 to 200,000 killed or missing, compared to Finland's approximately 25,000 casualties. The war ended with the Moscow Peace Treaty on March 12, 1940. Finland was forced to cede territories to the Soviet Union, including Karelia, which significantly altered its borders. However, Finland maintained its independence and sovereignty. While the war only led to sympathies by the United States, Norway, and Sweden, it did not directly impact the overall war. After World War 2, Finland maintained a delicate balancing act during the Cold War, pursuing a policy of neutrality while maintaining democratic institutions. Finland's successful post-war development is often referred to as the "Finnish Miracle."

Battle of France

May 10 - June 25, 1940

The Battle of France, which took place from May 10 to June 25, 1940, was a significant and dramatic early battle in World War 2 and the second major German invasion following the invasion of Poland. The Battle of France witnessed the German forces' effective use of Blitzkrieg tactics, emphasizing fast-moving armored divisions, combined arms, and close air support. This rapid and coordinated approach allowed the Germans to bypass heavily fortified areas and encircle the French and British forces. The battle was also marked by the apparent proportionality of forces. Germany's invading force consisted of approximately 3 million troops, while France and its British allies had a combined force of around 3.3 million. However, despite numerical parity, the Germans achieved surprise and mobility that proved decisive. The German invasion featured a significant breakthrough in the Ardennes Forest, a region considered impassable for tanks. The Germans exploited weaknesses in the French defenses, leading to the encirclement of a substantial portion of the French and British armies.

The Dunkirk Evacuation was a significant feature of the battle. As the German forces closed in on the trapped Allied Forces, from May 26 to June 4, 1940, a massive evacuation effort rescued over 330,000 British and French soldiers from the beaches of Dunkirk and brought them safely back to Britain.

However, the Germans were able to enter Paris on June 14, 1940 successfully, and the French government surrendered on June 22, 1940, effectively ending the Battle of France. The French capital remained under German occupation until 1944. Following the surrender, France was divided into occupied and unoccupied zones. The Vichy government, led by Marshal Philippe Pétain, governed the unoccupied zone and collaborated with the Germans. The Free French, led by Charles de Gaulle, continued to resist from abroad. The battle gave a significant moral boost to Germany, as it occupied large parts of Western Europe, including Belgium, the Netherlands, and Luxembourg. Overall, the Battle of France had significant strategic implications. It resulted in the collapse of one of the major Western European powers and allowed Germany to consolidate its position on the continent. The battle set the stage for the Battle of Britain and the broader conflict in Europe during World War 2.

Battle of Britain

July 10 - October 31, 1940

The Battle of Britain was a significant aerial conflict between the British Royal Air Force (RAF) and the German Luftwaffe during World War 2. It was part of the broader air campaign waged by Nazi Germany to gain air superiority over the British Isles and prepare for a possible invasion of Britain, codenamed Operation Sea Lion. The battle is commonly divided into three phases, with the first phase, known as the "Channel Battles," beginning on July 10, 1940, as German forces intensified their air raids on shipping convoys and coastal targets. The battle primarily involved the German Luftwaffe, led by Hermann Göring, and the British RAF, commanded by Air Chief Marshal Sir Hugh Dowding. The RAF carefully defended the British airspace against the Luftwaffe's bombing raids and attempts to gain air supremacy. The primary strategic targets for the Luftwaffe were the RAF airfields, radar installations, and aircraft factories. The destruction of these targets was intended to cripple the RAF's ability to defend British airspace. The second phase of the battle, known as "Eagle Attack," began on August 13, 1940. During this phase, the Luftwaffe shifted its focus to attacking RAF airfields and infrastructure to weaken the British air defenses. Despite heavy losses, the RAF and its pilots displayed tremendous determination and bravery. The British used their radar systems' advantages, effective communication, and well-coordinated tactics to repel German attacks. The battle reached a turning point on September 15, 1940, often called the "Battle of Britain Day." On this day, the Luftwaffe launched a massive air assault against London, diverting its focus from the RAF airfields. The RAF successfully defended the city, and the heavy losses suffered by the Luftwaffe forced it to shift its strategy. Recognizing the effectiveness of the

RAF's defense, the Luftwaffe shifted its focus to night bombing raids on British cities, marking the beginning of the Blitz. This shift allowed the RAF some respite and time to rebuild its forces. By October 31, 1940, the Luftwaffe had effectively abandoned its plans to invade Britain, and the Battle of Britain was considered won by the RAF. The battle demonstrated that air supremacy could not be easily achieved and marked a significant turning point in the war. In retrospect, however, the battle was costly for both sides. The RAF lost around 1,023 aircraft, while the Luftwaffe lost approximately 1,887 aircraft.

The Battle of Britain is remembered as a symbol of British resistance and resilience during World War 2. It not only thwarted Hitler's plans for an invasion of Britain but was also a crucial factor in the final defeat of Nazi Germany.

North African Campaign

1940 – 1943

The North African Campaign took place from 1940 to 1943 and was a series of battles and campaigns fought between the Axis powers and the Allied powers in the North African theater of World War 2. The Axis side consisted primarily of Germany and Italy, and the Allied powers mainly of the United Kingdom and Commonwealth forces. The campaign consisted of several theaters of operations, with the main battle zones being the Western Desert (Libya and Egypt), Eastern Desert (Egypt and Italian-occupied Ethiopia), and the Tunisia Campaign. It began in September 1940 when Italian forces from Libya, led by Marshal Rodolfo Graziani, invaded British-controlled Egypt but were subsequently defeated by the British Commonwealth forces. In December 1940, the British launched Operation Compass, a successful offensive that pushed the Italians back into Libya and captured tens of thousands of prisoners. British and Commonwealth forces advanced deep into Libya. In early 1941, Nazi Germany dispatched the Afrika Korps, led by General Erwin Rommel, to support the Italian troops in North Africa. Rommel's leadership and tactical skills earned him the nickname "The Desert Fox." The North African Campaign saw a series of back-and-forth battles, with both sides gaining and losing ground. Key battles included Gazala, Tobruk, and El Alamein. The Second Battle of El Alamein in October 1942 marked a central turning point in the campaign. Allied forces received significant reinforcements, including troops from the United States and the Free French under General Charles de Gaulle. American tanks, equipment, and supplies played a crucial role in the campaign. In November 1942, the Allied forces launched Operation Torch, an amphibious invasion of French North Africa (Morocco, Algeria, and Tunisia). This operation marked the beginning of the end for Axis forces in North Africa. By May 1943, the remaining Axis forces in North Africa, including German and Italian troops, surrendered to the Allies. The campaign ended with the capture of nearly 250,000 Axis prisoners.

The North African Campaign had several significant consequences. It demonstrated the effectiveness of combined arms operations and improved Allied coordination. It also diverted Axis resources from other theaters like the Eastern Front. The defeat of Axis forces in North Africa was a significant blow to their overall war effort. The campaign's legacy extended beyond the war itself. The experiences of many officers in the North Africa campaign, including Dwight D. Eisenhower, George S. Patton, and Bernard Montgomery, would play a vital role in their leadership during the later stages of World War 2 in Europe.

Operation Barbarossa

June 22, 1941

Operation Barbarossa, launched by Nazi Germany on June 22, 1941, was the largest military operation in history up to that point and marked the beginning of the Eastern Front in World War 2. Operation Barbarossa was essentially a codename for the German invasion of the Soviet Union. Adolf Hitler and the German High Command sought to conquer vast territories of the Soviet Union, eliminate the Soviet state, and secure resources, especially oil, for Germany's war effort. The operation involved deploying approximately 4.5 million German and Axis troops along a front that stretched from the Arctic Circle in the north to the Black Sea in the south, making it the largest invasion force in history. German troops were able to achieve rapid success in the opening phases of the campaign. They encircled and captured hundreds of thousands of Soviet troops and advanced deep into Soviet territory. Key objectives of the operation included capturing Leningrad (now Saint Petersburg), Moscow, and Kyiv. Leningrad was besieged, Moscow was approached, and Kyiv was occupied during the campaign. However, the Battle of Moscow (October 1941 to January 1942) was a turning point in the campaign. The Soviet defense of Moscow halted the German advance, marking it the first significant defeat for the Wehrmacht. As the campaign continued into 1942, it evolved into a war of attrition. Both sides suffered heavy casualties, with millions of soldiers killed, wounded, or captured.

Pearl Harbor

December 7, 1941

The attack on Pearl Harbor, which occurred on December 7, 1941, served as a major transformative event in World War 2 and led to the United States' entry into the war. The attack on Pearl Harbor was a surprise military attack on the U.S. naval base at Pearl Harbor, Hawaii, by the Imperial Japanese Navy. The attack had come without a formal declaration of war. The Japanese forces attacked on the morning of December 7, 1941. It began at 7:48 a.m. Hawaiian time and continued for nearly two hours. The primary objectives of the Japanese attack were to cripple the U.S. Pacific Fleet and prevent the United States from interfering in Japanese military operations in Southeast Asia. The attack aimed to destroy battleships, aircraft, and infrastructure at Pearl Harbor. The attack inflicted significant damage on the U.S. Pacific Fleet. Eight American battleships were either sunk or heavily damaged, including the USS Arizona, which exploded and sank with a considerable loss of lives. Several other ships were damaged, and nearly 200 aircraft were destroyed. The attack also resulted in a high number of casualties. Approximately 2,403 Americans were killed, and another 1,178 were wounded. Most of the deaths occurred on the USS Arizona.

President Franklin D. Roosevelt delivered his famous speech to Congress on December 8, 1941, one day after the Japanese attack on Pearl Harbor. This speech is often referred to as the "Day of Infamy" speech and was instrumental in galvanizing support for the United States' entry into World War 2. The same day, the United States declared war on Japan on December 8, 1941, marking the country's entry into World War 2. This move also initiated the Pacific Theater of World War 2, with the United States and its allies engaging in a prolonged conflict against Japan in the Pacific.

Battle of Stalingrad

August 23, 1942 - February 2, 1943

The Battle of Stalingrad was a significant and brutal battle lasting approximately five and a half months. It was a major offensive by Nazi Germany to capture Stalingrad and gain control of critical resources and transportation routes in the Soviet Union. The battle was marked by extreme brutality, with both sides suffering heavy casualties. Street-to-street, house-to-house combat, and close-quarters fighting were common, leading to high casualties and significant destruction. The Soviet defenders employed a strategy of stubborn resistance, refusing to give up the city, even when surrounded. They built an extensive network of trenches, fortifications, and defensive positions. The Germans managed to encircle Stalingrad in late 1942, trapping the Soviet defenders inside the city. This encirclement was known as the "cauldron" or "kessel."

However, in late November 1942, the Soviet Union launched a massive counteroffensive, Operation Uranus, which aimed to encircle the encircling German forces. This operation succeeded in cutting off the Germans and their allies from their supply lines. On January 31, 1943, realizing their dire situation and running out of supplies, General Friedrich Paulus and his German forces surrendered to the Soviet Union. This move was a significant humiliation for the German Army and indicated a turning point in the Eastern Front of World War 2.

Battle of Midway

June 4-7, 1942

The Battle of Midway took place from June 4 to June 7, 1942. It was a naval battle in the Pacific where the United States defeated Japanese forces, halting Japanese expansion. The battle occurred near the Midway Atoll, a small group of islands in the central Pacific Ocean. The Midway Atoll was a strategic outpost for both the United States and Japan. The battle was a resounding victory for the United States, marked the first significant defeat of the Japanese Navy, and halted their expansion in the Pacific. The battle is often considered the turning point in the Pacific War.

Battle of Guadalcanal

August 7, 1942 - February 9, 1943

The Battle of Guadalcanal was another critical campaign between Japanese and U.S. forces in the Pacific theater of World War 2. Guadalcanal was strategically significant because it was home to a Japanese airfield (Henderson Field) that threatened the sea lanes between the United States and Australia. The control of this airfield was crucial for both sides. The campaign saw a series of naval battles, including the Battle of the Eastern Solomons (August 24-25, 1942) and the Battle of Cape Esperance (October 11-12, 1942). These engagements resulted in losses on both sides but ultimately allowed the United States to maintain control of Henderson Field. The battle on Guadalcanal involved intense jungle warfare, with both sides suffering from disease, harsh conditions, and determined enemy forces. The U.S. Marines endured a protracted struggle to hold the island against Japanese counterattacks. By early 1943, the Japanese decided to withdraw their remaining forces from Guadalcanal due to heavy losses and an inability to resupply their troops effectively. The United States claimed victory in the campaign.

Battle of Kursk

July 5 - August 23, 1943

The Battle of Kursk was one of history's largest and most significant tank battles. It took place near Kursk in western Russia, specifically in the Kursk Salient, a bulge in the front lines, and was fought between the German and Soviet armies. The German Army, led by Field Marshal Erich von Manstein and Field Marshal Gunther von Kluge, launched the offensive known as Operation Citadel, while the Red Army, under the command of Marshal Georgy Zhukov and Marshal Konstantin Rokossovsky, successfully defended against the German attack.

The Germans aimed to eliminate the Kursk Salient, a Soviet defensive bulge, and regain the initiative on the Eastern Front. Controlling Kursk would allow the Germans to threaten Moscow and cut off Soviet forces in the salient. The Soviets had months to prepare for the German offensive. They constructed extensive defensive fortifications, including trenches, minefields, and anti-tank obstacles. They also deployed a vast number of troops, tanks, and artillery pieces. The Battle of Kursk is often remembered for the colossal tank battles that occurred during the engagement. It featured large-scale tank clashes between German Panzer divisions and Soviet tank corps.

Overall, the Battle of Kursk resulted in a strategic stalemate. The Germans were unable to achieve their objectives, and the Soviet counteroffensive gradually pushed them back. By late August, the Red Army had retaken most of the lost territory. Its outcome of a stalemate marked a turning point on the Eastern Front of

World War 2. This was the last major German offensive in the east, and after their defeat, the Soviet Union gained the initiative and began pushing the German forces westward. It demonstrated the effectiveness of Soviet defensive preparations, marked the decline of German offensive capabilities on the Eastern Front, and is notable for its role in shaping the course of the war in Eastern Europe. The battle set the stage for the series of Soviet offensives that would finally lead to the liberation of Eastern Europe and the final defeat of Nazi Germany in 1945.

Invasion of Sicily

July 9 - August 17, 1943

The Invasion of Sicily, also known as Operation Husky, was a major Allied military campaign whose primary objective was to liberate the island of Sicily, which was then under German and Italian occupation. Sicily was strategically important because of its location in the Mediterranean, and its capture would pave the way for the Allied takeover of mainland Italy. The operation was conducted by a coalition of Allied forces, primarily American, British, and Canadian troops. General Dwight D. Eisenhower served as the Supreme Commander of the Allied Expeditionary Force. The defending forces included German and Italian troops, with Field Marshal Albert Kesselring overseeing the Axis defense.

Operation Husky involved a massive amphibious assault on the southern coast of Sicily. Troops were landed on a series of beaches, including the Gulf of Gela, to establish a foothold on the island. Before the amphibious landings, Allied paratroopers and glider-borne troops were dropped behind enemy lines to disrupt communication and impede the movement of Axis reinforcements. Despite initial resistance from German and Italian forces, the Allies made rapid progress inland, capturing key cities and towns. The Allies advanced steadily and captured the city of Messina on August 17, 1943, marking the end of the Sicilian campaign. Messina's capture effectively severed Sicily from the Italian mainland. In the face of the Allied advance, the remaining German and Italian forces withdrew from Sicily to the Italian mainland. The evacuation was conducted under pressure, and substantial equipment and personnel were lost. Overall, Operation Husky demonstrated the successful coordination of Allied forces, including land, air, and naval components. It served as a precursor to the more extensive Allied campaigns in Italy and the eventual liberation of Western Europe.

D-Day (Operation Overlord)

June 6, 1944

D-Day, or Operation Overlord, was the Allied invasion of Normandy, France, on June 6, 1944, during World War 2. It marked the beginning of the liberation of Western Europe from Nazi occupation. The primary objective of D-Day was to establish a beachhead in Normandy and secure a foothold for the Allied forces to launch a larger offensive against Nazi-occupied Western Europe. The operation was conducted by a coalition of Allied forces, primarily consisting of American, British, Canadian, and Free French troops. As Commander-in-Chief of the Allied Expeditionary Force during the Invasion of Sicily, amongst several other encounters, General Dwight D. Eisenhower still commanded the Allied army during Operation Overlord.

D-Day involved a massive amphibious assault, with Allied troops landing on the beaches of Normandy. The landing zones were divided into five sectors: Utah, Omaha, Gold, Juno, and Sword. In the hours preceding the beach landings, Allied paratroopers and glider-borne troops were dropped down behind enemy lines to secure key objectives, disrupt German defenses, and clear the way for the amphibious assault. The Allies employed an elaborate deception campaign known as Operation Fortitude to mislead the Germans about the location and timing of the invasion. Fake radio traffic, dummy equipment, and misinformation were used to confuse the enemy. Despite strong German defenses, the Allies successfully established beachheads at all five landing zones. The most challenging and costly assault was on Omaha Beach, where American forces faced heavy resistance and suffered significant casualties. Once the beachheads were secured, Allied troops began breaking out and advancing inland. Over the following weeks and months, they liberated occupied France and pushed eastward.

The D-Day is often considered a turning point in World War 2. It opened up a second front in Western Europe, relieving pressure on the Eastern Front, where the Soviet Union was already engaged in heavy fighting against Nazi Germany. The operation also marked the beginning of the liberation of Western Europe from Nazi occupation. It set the stage for the eventual defeat of Nazi Germany and the end of World War 2 in Europe.

Battle of the Bulge

December 16, 1944 - January 25, 1945

The Battle of the Bulge, also called the Ardennes Counteroffensive, took place in the Ardennes region of Belgium, Luxembourg, and northeastern France. The primary Allied forces involved were the United States, the United Kingdom, and Belgium, with the U.S. First Army, U.S. Ninth Army, and British XXX Corps among the units engaged. The German Army, led by Field Marshal Gerd von Rundstedt and supported by the Sixth SS Panzer Army, spearheaded the offensive. The battle began with a massive German surprise attack against thinly defended sections of the Allied front. The Germans hoped to split the Allied lines, capture the Belgian port of Antwerp, and potentially force the Western Allies to have to negotiate a separate peace. The German offensive initially achieved significant success, creating a 50-mile-deep salient in the Allied lines. They captured several key towns and inflicted heavy casualties on American forces. Despite being caught off guard, the Allied forces rallied and put up fierce resistance. General George S. Patton's Third Army played a critical role in relieving the besieged town of Bastogne.

By late January 1945, the Germans were forced to retreat, having failed to achieve their objectives. The Battle of the Bulge had exacted a heavy toll on both sides but marked a significant Allied victory.

Eastern Front

1944 - 1945

During World War 2, the Eastern Front saw significant developments in 1944-1945, as the tide of the war turned against Nazi Germany. In 1944, the Soviet Red Army launched a series of massive offensives on the Eastern Front, pushing German forces westward. These offensives included Operation Bagration (June 1944), which liberated Belarus, and Operation August Storm (August 1945), which resulted in the Soviet occupation of Manchuria and the Kuril Islands. The Soviet advances in 1944-1945 led to the liberation of large parts of Eastern Europe from Nazi occupation. Countries such as Poland, Hungary, Czechoslovakia, and Romania were freed from German control. As the Red Army advanced westward, it became clear that the ultimate prize was Berlin, the capital of Nazi Germany.

The Allies, particularly the Soviets and the Western Allies, raced to reach and capture the city.

In February 1945, the leaders of the Allied powers—Winston Churchill (United Kingdom), Franklin D. Roosevelt (United States), and Joseph Stalin (Soviet Union)—met at the Yalta Conference. They discussed the division of Germany and the future of Eastern Europe after the war. In April 1945, Soviet forces launched a final assault on Berlin. The city fell to the Red Army on May 2, 1945, marking the effective end of Nazi Germany. Adolf Hitler had committed suicide in his bunker a few days earlier.

Victory in Europe (VE) Day, celebrating the surrender of Nazi Germany, was celebrated on May 8, 1945, in most Western Allied countries and on May 9, 1945, in the Soviet Union. This surrender marked the official end of World War 2 in Europe.

Iwo Jima

February 19 - March 26, 1945

The Battle of Iwo Jima was a major battle fought in the Pacific Theatre between the United States and Japanese forces. Iwo Jima was a strategically important target for the United States because it could serve as an emergency landing strip for damaged B-29 bombers on their way back from bombing raids on Japan. It also provided early warning radar stations for the Japanese. The Japanese had heavily fortified the island with an extensive network of tunnels, bunkers, and underground positions. They were prepared to engage in a prolonged defense, making it a difficult target for the Americans. The battle for Iwo Jima was characterized by intense and brutal combat. The Marines faced determined Japanese resistance and suffered heavy casualties. Following an amphibious assault, the U.S. Marines landed on Iwo Jima's beaches under heavy Japanese fire. One of the most iconic moments of the battle was the raising of the American flag on Mount Suribachi by a group of Marines on February 23, 1945. This event was captured in a famous photograph by Joe Rosenthal and symbolized the spirit and determination of American forces.

Atomic bombings of Hiroshima and Nagasaki

August 6 and 9, 1945

On 6 and 9 August 1945, the United States set off two atomic bombs over two Japanese cities, Hiroshima and Nagasaki. The bombings led to between 129,000 and 226,000 deaths, mostly civilians, and remain the only time nuclear weapons have been used in an armed conflict. Japan surrendered to the Allied forces on August 15, six days after the attack on Nagasaki, the Soviet Union's announcement of war against Japan, and the invasion of Japanese-occupied Manchuria.

The war in the European theatre ended when Germany surrendered on May 8, 1945, and the Allied forces turned their focus to the Pacific War. By July 1945, the Allied forces' Manhattan Project had created two different atomic bombs. The first was called "Little Boy", an enriched uranium gun-type fission weapon. The second one was called "Fat Man", a plutonium implosion-type nuclear weapon. The U.S. Army Air Forces' 509th Composite Group was trained and outfitted with the specialized Silverplate edition of the Boeing B-29 Superfortress and deployed to Tinian in the Mariana Islands. In the Potsdam Declaration on July 26, 1945, the Allied forces requested the total surrender of the Imperial Japanese armed forces, with the alternative being "prompt and utter destruction". The Japanese command ignored the ultimatum.

As required by the Quebec Agreement, consent for the bombing was obtained from the United Kingdom, and on July 25, the acting chief of staff of the U.S. Army, General Thomas Handy, issued orders for atomic bombs to be used on Hiroshima, Kokura, Niigata, and Nagasaki. These targets were selected because they were large urban areas with important military facilities. On August 6, a Little Boy was dropped over Hiroshima. Three days later, a Fat Man was dropped over Nagasaki. Over the next two to four months, the aftermath of the atomic bombings led to between 90,000 and 146,000 deaths in Hiroshima and 60,000 and 80,000 deaths in Nagasaki. About half of the deaths occurred on the first day. For months, people continued to die from the effects of radiation, burns, injuries, and sickness, compounded by malnutrition and illness. Though Hiroshima had a large armed forces, most of the dead were civilians.

3

LEADERS OF
WORLD WAR 2

From Winston Churchill's inspiring speeches to Adolf Hitler's destructive policies, each leader played a unique and significant role in the unfolding drama of global conflict. In this chapter, we delve into the lives and roles of key leaders of both – the Allied and Axis powers - who shaped the course of World War 2.

Allied Powers

Winston Churchill

Winston Churchill was a prominent leader during World War 2 and is often remembered as one of the key figures in the Allied victory over Nazi Germany. He served as the Prime Minister of the United Kingdom, first from 1940 to 1945 and then again from 1951 to 1955. He assumed the role of Prime Minister during a critical time in the war when the United Kingdom faced the threat of invasion by Nazi Germany. Churchill was known for his powerful and inspirational speeches that rallied the British people and their allies during the darkest days of the war. His speeches, including the famous "We shall fight on the beaches" address, bolstered morale and determination in the face of adversity. Churchill was known for his unwavering determination to resist Nazi aggression. He famously stated, "We shall never surrender," emphasizing the British resolve to continue fighting until victory was achieved.

Churchill played a crucial role in building and maintaining the Allied coalition. He worked closely with the other Allied leaders, such as U.S. President Franklin D. Roosevelt and Soviet Premier Joseph Stalin, to coordinate the war effort and develop joint strategies. Churchill was deeply involved in military strategy and planning. He participated in high-level discussions and decisions about the conduct of the war, including the timing and location of major offensives. He actively supported resistance movements in occupied Europe and championed the idea of "setting Europe ablaze" through sabotage, espionage, and guerrilla warfare. This support helped weaken the Nazi regime from within.

Moreover, Churchill played a significant role in post-war diplomacy, including the negotiations at the Yalta and Potsdam Conferences. These conferences shaped the post-war world and established the groundwork for the United Nations.

After the war, Churchill continued to be an essential figure in international politics. He delivered his memorable "Iron Curtain" speech in 1946, warning of the division of Europe and the growing influence of the Soviet Union.

Franklin D. Roosevelt

Franklin D. Roosevelt, often referred to as FDR, was a key leader during World War 2 and served as the president of the United States throughout most of the war. To begin with, Roosevelt was the only U.S. president to serve four terms, with his tenure spanning from 1933 to 1945. He provided steady and determined leadership during one of the most challenging periods in American history. FDR played a pivotal role in building and maintaining the Allied coalition, which included the United States, the United Kingdom, the Soviet Union, and other nations. He championed the Lend-Lease Act, which allowed the United States to provide vital military aid, including equipment, supplies, and food, to Allied nations without immediate payment. This program significantly bolstered the war efforts of Britain, the Soviet Union, and other Allies.

His vision of the United States as the "Arsenal of Democracy" emphasized America's role in producing vast quantities of war material, from tanks and aircraft to ships and ammunition, to support the Allies. He led the United States through the shock and devastation of the Japanese attack on Pearl Harbor on December 7, 1941. The following day, he delivered his famous "Day of Infamy" speech, leading to the U.S. declaration of war on Japan and its entry into WWII.

Roosevelt's achievements regarding war production and mobilization are noteworthy. Under his leadership, the United States rapidly transformed its economy into a wartime production powerhouse. The war effort led to full employment and a remarkable industrial output that contributed significantly to the Allied victory. He initiated the top-secret Manhattan Project, which ultimately developed the atomic bomb.

Roosevelt was also involved in crucial wartime conferences, including the Atlantic Charter conference with Winston Churchill in 1941, where they outlined their vision for a post-war world based on democratic principles and self-determination. He also participated in the Cairo, Tehran, and Yalta Conferences with Allied leaders. His vision for the post-war world included establishing the United Nations, an international organization aiming to promote peace and cooperation among nations. He played a vital role in the development of the UN Charter.

Joseph Stalin

Joseph Stalin was the General Secretary of the Communist Party of the Soviet Union and the country's de facto leader during World War 2. Under his leadership, the Soviet Union emerged as one of the key Allied powers in the fight against Nazi Germany. In August 1939, Stalin signed the Molotov-Ribbentrop Pact with Nazi Germany, including a secret protocol that divided Eastern Europe into spheres of influence. This pact allowed the Soviets to remain neutral in the early stages of the war while Germany invaded Poland and Western Europe.

However, despite the non-aggression pact, Nazi Germany violated it by launching Operation Barbarossa on June 22, 1941, and invading the Soviet Union. Stalin's response to the invasion was to mobilize the Soviet people for a determined defense against the German onslaught. To impede the German advance, Stalin implemented a scorched earth policy, ordering the destruction of infrastructure, resources, and supplies that could be of use to the invading forces. This policy contributed to the difficulties faced by the German army during the harsh Russian winter.

Stalin and the Soviet leadership adopted a policy of "total war," mobilizing the entire Soviet population for the war effort. This move included the conscription of millions of soldiers and mobilizing women and civilians to work in war-related industries. He also played a significant role in the strategic planning of major battles, including the Battle of Stalingrad (1942-1943) and the Battle of Kursk (1943), both turning points in the war on the Eastern Front.

However, Stalin's leadership came at a significant human cost. The Soviet Union suffered immense casualties during the war, where millions of soldiers and civilians were killed or wounded.

Chiang Kai-shek

Chiang Kai-shek was the leader of the Republic of China (ROC) and the head of the Kuomintang (KMT) political party. Chiang Kai-shek and the ROC government were at the forefront of the Chinese resistance against Japanese aggression in the lead-up to and during World War 2. Japan invaded Manchuria in 1931 and launched a full-scale invasion of China in 1937, leading to the Second Sino-Japanese War. Chiang Kai-shek sought support from the Western Allies, particularly the United States, in resisting Japanese aggression. The United States aided the ROC through the Lend-Lease program, which included supplies, equipment, and financial support.

He played a crucial role in forming a United Front against Japan, which included cooperation with the Chinese Communist Party (CCP) led by Mao Zedong. Despite the ongoing Chinese Civil War between the KMT and CCP, the United Front aimed to unite all Chinese forces against the common enemy, Japan.

Charles de Gaulle

Charles de Gaulle was a prominent French military officer and statesman who served as the leader of the Free French Forces. His achievements were notable and had a lasting impact on France and its role in the war. After the surrender of France to Nazi Germany in 1940, de Gaulle refused to accept the armistice and the collaborationist Vichy government. On June 18, 1940, he made a famous radio broadcast from London, calling on the French people to resist the occupation and continue the fight against the Axis powers.

De Gaulle's insistence on not recognizing the Vichy regime and his unwavering commitment to the cause of a free France helped him establish his legitimacy as a leader. Over time, many French colonies, individual soldiers, and resistance fighters rallied to his call. He played an important role in rallying support from French colonies in North Africa, particularly Algeria. Through diplomatic efforts and persuasion, he managed to secure the allegiance of General Henri Giraud, another French officer in North Africa, thereby strengthening the Free French cause.

He also worked tirelessly to build strong relationships with the Allied powers, especially the United States and the United Kingdom. Given his tenacity and diplomacy, he ensured that the French Free Forces were recognized as legitimate partners of the Allied Forces. As a key military leader, he played a significant role in the liberation of French North and West Africa and later in the liberation of France itself. As a political leader beyond the battlefield, he played a crucial role in the political negotiations that followed the liberation of France, helping to shape the nation's post-war destiny. In 1944, he established the Provisional Government of the French Republic and later served as the first president of the French Fourth Republic.

One of his goals was to restore French sovereignty and ensure France would have a voice in the post-war world order. In this regard, he played a crucial role in establishing the United Nations.

Harry S. Truman

Harry S. Truman was the 33rd president of the United States, who assumed office on April 12, 1945, a few months before the end of World War 2.

Perhaps the most significant decision Truman made during WWII was the authorization of the use of atomic bombs on the Japanese cities of Hiroshima and Nagasaki in August 1945. He decided to use these devastating weapons after consulting with his advisors and considering the alternatives. The bombings ultimately led to Japan's surrender and the end of the war in the Pacific.

Truman also participated in the Potsdam Conference, which took place in July and August 1945. This conference included discussions between the leaders of the Allied powers (the United States, the Soviet Union, and the United Kingdom) about the post-war administration of Germany and the terms of Japan's surrender. The conference helped set the stage for the post-war order. He was instrumental in founding the United Nations (UN), an international organization established to promote peace and cooperation among nations. Following the end of WWII, Truman oversaw the demobilization of the U.S. military and the country's transition from a wartime economy to a peacetime one. This complex task involved addressing issues such as the return of veterans, reconversion of industries, and the challenges of post-war diplomacy.

Axis Powers

Adolf Hitler

Hitler played a central and destructive role during World War 2. It would be fair to suggest that his actions and policies were a significant reason behind the outbreak of the war in the first place. He had aggressive expansionist policies as he sought to overturn the Treaty of Versailles, which had imposed severe restrictions on Germany following World War 1. In violation of international agreements, Hitler ordered the reoccupation of the Rhineland in

1936, followed by the annexation of Austria (Anschluss) in 1938 and the dismemberment of Czechoslovakia in 1938-1939. In 1939, he ordered the invasion of Poland, marking the official beginning of World War 2. This invasion triggered the response of France and the United Kingdom, leading to a broader conflict.

One of the most chilling aspects of Hitler's role in WWII was his implementation of the Holocaust. Under his leadership, the Nazi regime systematically murdered around six million Jews, as well as millions of others, including Romani people, disabled individuals, political dissidents, and more. Concentration camps and extermination camps were established to carry out these atrocities.

Heinrich Himmler

Heinrich Himmler played a prominent and sinister role during World War 2 as one of the key figures in Nazi Germany's leadership. As the head of the Schutzstaffel (SS) and various other organizations, Himmler was instrumental in implementing the Holocaust and overseeing various aspects of Nazi Germany's war effort.

He held the title of Reichsführer-SS, making him the highest-ranking officer in the SS, a paramilitary organization initially tasked with providing security for Adolf Hitler and other high-ranking Nazis. Under Himmler's leadership, the SS grew into a vast and powerful organization with influence over numerous aspects of the Nazi regime. Himmler oversaw the construction and operation of the concentration and extermination camps, including Auschwitz, Sobibor, and Treblinka. He appointed individuals like Rudolf Höss to manage these camps, where mass murders, forced labor, and inhumane experiments occurred. Himmler was a fervent believer in Nazi racial ideology and pursued a program of eugenics to maintain a "pure" Aryan race (Barrowclough, 2017). He promoted the SS as a racially elite group and initiated programs to encourage selective breeding among its members.

Benito Mussolini

Benito Mussolini played a significant role during World War 2 as the leader of Italy and a key Axis power alongside Nazi Germany and Japan. In April 1939, Mussolini ordered the invasion of Albania, a relatively easy victory for Italian forces. This expansion marked Italy's first territorial conquest in World War 2 and was intended to demonstrate Mussolini's imperial ambitions. Italy entered World War 2 on the Axis side by invading France in 1940. However, the Italian campaign was largely ineffective and did not achieve significant territorial gains, especially compared to the rapid success of the German invasion. Mussolini also directed Italian forces to participate in the North African theatre of the war, where they clashed with British and Commonwealth troops under the command of General Erwin Rommel. The Italian military's performance in North Africa was generally lackluster, and suffered significant defeats.

By 1943, Italy's military situation had deteriorated significantly. Mussolini was arrested, and the Fascist government fell from power. Italy then signed an armistice with the Allies in September 1943, effectively switching sides in the war. The Germans subsequently occupied much of Italy, and Mussolini was rescued by German forces and established a puppet state in Northern Italy known as the Italian Social Republic.

Hideki Tojo

Hideki Tojo played a crucial role as Japan's Prime Minister and the Japanese government's chief military leader during World War 2.

He was appointed Japan's Prime Minister in October 1941, a position he held until July 1944. He was a high-ranking military officer and a member of the Imperial Japanese Army, holding various key positions before becoming Prime Minister. Tojo strongly advocated for Japan's expansionist policies in East Asia and the Pacific. Under his leadership, Japan continued its aggressive expansion by invading and occupying territories such as Manchuria (1931), China (1937), French Indochina (1940), and various Pacific islands.

Tojo was instrumental in planning and executing the surprise attack on the U.S. naval base at Pearl Harbor, Hawaii, on December 7, 1941. This attack resulted in the United States entering World War 2 and initiated the Pacific theater of the conflict.

Emperor Hirohito

Emperor Hirohito of Japan played a complex and symbolic role during World War 2. He was the constitutional monarch of Japan and held a unique position in the government and society. The Japanese constitution granted him a largely ceremonial role, and he was expected to follow the advice of his government and Cabinet ministers. Nevertheless, he held great symbolic importance as the symbol of the Japanese state and unity. During World War 2, he played a symbolic role in promoting Japan's militaristic and expansionist agenda. He appeared in propaganda materials and ceremonies to bolster public support for the war effort.

4

ALLIED POWERS VS. AXIS POWERS

A s discussed in our earlier chapters, the Second World War saw the formation of two main alliances: the Allies and the Axis. This chapter will shed light on the ideologies, strategies, and strengths and weaknesses of the two main alliances during the war.

Ideologies

Allies: The Allies primarily comprised a coalition of nations, the major ones of whom included the United States, the United Kingdom, and the Soviet Union. Their ideology and purpose of war was centered around the values of liberal democracy, freedom, and opposition to fascist regimes like Nazi Germany and Imperial Japan.

Axis: The Axis, on the other hand, was led by Nazi Germany under Adolf Hitler, Italy under Benito Mussolini, and Japan under Emperor Hirohito. Their ideologies were characterized by fascism, militarism, and expansionism. Moreover, Hitler's policy on the holocaust and sentiments of anti-Semitism also served at the heart of his ideology, which opposed the ideals of the Allies.

Strategies

Allies: The Allies adopted a strategy of "Europe First," focusing on defeating Hitler's Nazi Germany before turning their complete attention towards the Japanese threat in the east. Their plan included a combination of military tactics, such as the "Western Front" and the "Eastern Front" in Europe, and military campaigns in the Pacific against the Imperial Japanese forces. Moreover, the Allies also employed a range of strategic bombing campaigns to disrupt the war efforts of the Axis forces and destroy industrial and civilian infrastructures. These operations were mostly well-coordinated under the leadership of military leaders like U.S. General Dwight Eisenhower.

Axis: Germany used various tactics, such as the blitzkrieg (lightning war) strategy, to swiftly conquer neighboring countries such as Poland. They used superior tanks such as to conduct fast-moving and highly coordinated attacks. On the other hand, Japan sought to expand its empire in the Asia-Pacific region through several aggressive military campaigns. It partially succeeded in doing so, taking over Manila (Philipines), Singapore, and the Dutch East Indies. The Axis powers did collaborate to some extent but did not have the same level of coordination as the Allies.

Strengths

Allies: The Allies, especially the United States, had a vast range of economic and industrial resources, which allowed them to produce large amounts of weapons, equipment, and supplies. Moreover, they had a broad and diverse coalition of nations, which brought together different strengths, including the Soviet Union's manpower and the naval prowess of the British Royal Navy. Technological innovation was another key strength of the Allies, as they had developed advanced military technologies such as the Enigma machine (code-breaking), radar, and the atomic bomb, amongst others.

Axis: The Axis powers were able to achieve some victories earlier on in the war. These victories included Germany's swift overthrow of Poland, France, and much of Europe. On the Asian front, the Japanese also made significant territorial gains, such as in Manila and Singapore. While Germany possessed relatively advanced military technology regarding tank warfare and aircraft, Japan had a highly skilled and disciplined infantry.

Weaknesses

Allied: The first major challenge for the Allies was related to co-ordination: it was an uphill task to manage a coalition of nations with different objectives and strategies, which required effective diplomacy. Furthermore, there are significant logistical challenges pertaining to supplying and maintaining armies over vast distances, especially in the Pacific region. Moreover, the Allies suffered significant defeats in the early years of the war, such as the fall of France in 1940 and the attack on Pearl Harbor in 1941, which exposed significant weaknesses in their military readiness.

Axis: The Axis powers faced challenges maintaining control over vast conquered territories, leading to logistical problems and resistance movements. Moreover, they were at a significant economic disadvantage compared to the Allies. Germany faced resource shortages as the war continued. Besides, differences in objectives and ideologies among the Axis members sometimes hindered effective collaboration.

Comparison of Military Strength

Manpower

Allied: The Soviet Union had an extensive pool of manpower of up to 34 million soldiers, which contributed significantly to the overall physical strength of the Allies. Besides, the United States and the British Commonwealth nations could mobilize substantial armies given their better coordination and technology. The physical forces of the Allied forces also included resistance movements in occupied territories, which actively took part in guerrilla warfare.

Axis: Germany had a large and well-trained army of about 13.6 million soldiers, which was further bolstered by the combat branch of the Nazi party, the Waffen-SS. Japan also had a highly disciplined and motivated military force of roughly 2.35 million soldiers.

Equipment and Technology

Allies: The Allies had a superior industrial capacity, enabling them to produce modern weapons and equipment. They were able to develop advanced technologies such as the atomic bomb (the Manhattan Project), radar, and the Enigma code-breaking machine, which helped them fight against Germany. Besides, the United States and the United Kingdom, in particular, had an effective and well-coordinated logistics system.

Axis: Germany had technologically advanced tanks like the Tiger and Panther tanks. The Axis powers developed the V-2 rocket and made advancements in jet propulsion technology, and Japan had advanced naval technology, particularly in aircraft carriers and torpedoes.

Industrial Capacity

Allies: The United States had the world's most extensive industrial base, which enabled the mass production of weapons and equipment. Although the Soviet Union faced initial setbacks, it could effectively mobilize its vast industrial resources.

Axis: Germany had a highly industrialized economy but faced resource shortages as the war continued. On the other hand, Japan had a limited industrial capacity in comparison to the United States and the Soviet Union.

5

RESISTANCE MOVEMENTS

There were various resistance movements throughout Europe during World War 2, which primarily aimed at resisting Nazi propaganda, occupation and oppression. These included the French Resistance, the Polish Home Army, and the Norwegian Resistance. In this chapter, we seek to discover some of the critical resistance movements and assess the degree to which they were successful.

French Resistance

The French Resistance, also known as La Résistance, emerged immediately after the capture of France by Nazi Germany in 1940. The resistance encompassed a wide range of groups and individuals from different political, social, and cultural backgrounds, and its primary goal was to undermine the German occupation, gather intelligence, and support the Allied forces. Moreover, the resistance fighters had excellent expertise in acts of sabotage, espionage, and other guerrilla warfare tactics.

Among the key leaders of the French Resistance was Jean Moulin, who played a crucial role in unifying various factions under a single umbrella. He was able to spearhead sabotage operations against transportation infrastructure, attacks on German military installations, and the collection of vital intelligence information. Moreover, they also helped Allied airmen in shooting down over France to escape to safety. Although the French Resistance was successful in many regards, it faced various challenges simultaneously. For instance, there was a constant threat of infiltration by the Nazi spies, and the Resistance leaders and members had to face brutal reprisals if discovered. Besides, their efforts were also often opposed by collaborationist Vichy French authorities.

Polish Home Army (Armia Krajowa)

The Polish Home Army was another critical resistance movement during the Second World War. It was established in 1942 and soon became one of the largest and most organized resistance movements across occupied Europe. In terms of its outlook, it was an underground army that was loyal to the Polish government in exile during the Nazi occupation.

The goals of the Polish Home Army included resistance to Nazi occupation and preparation for the eventual liberation of Poland. Like the French Resistance, they engaged in acts of sabotage and intelligence gathering and went on to try to liberate Warsaw during the Warsaw Uprising in 1944. Among some of the notable leaders of the Polish Home Army were Tadeusz Bór-Komorowski, Stefan Rowecki, and Jan Karski. Some of the other operations which the Home Army conducted included the assassinations of high-ranking Nazi officials, sabotage of German infrastructure, and intelligence gathering for the Allies.

However, it comes as no surprise that the Home Army faced severe repression by the Nazis, who sought to crush any form of resistance movement within Poland. While the Warsaw Uprising was heroic, it resulted in significant civilian casualties and left much of Warsaw in ruins.

Norwegian Resistance Movement

Through Operation Weserubung in 1940, Nazi Germany had been able to occupy much of Denmark and Norway. The resistance movement lasted from 1940 until 1945, when the Allied powers defeated Germany. One of the critical goals of the movement was to assert the legitimacy of the Norwegian leaders in exile and question the legitimacy of the pro-Nazi government led by Vidkun Quisling and Josef Terboven.

The resistance movement had initially been successful in Southern Norway, where, although disorganized, it successfully allowed the government to escape capture. On the other hand, it was more organized as a military organization in the Western and Northern parts of Norway, where it aimed to secure strategic positions and evacuate the government. The Norwegian resistance fighters were also known as the Milorg, and they conducted large-scale sabotage operations against Nazi installations. Moreover, they had good expertise in commando raids, assassinations as well as other special operations against the Nazi regime. Amongst a significant success was the destruction of heavy water production facilities, which were crucial for the Nazi atomic weapons program.

Danish Resistance

Similar to the Norwegian Resistance, The Danish Resistance also developed in response to the occupation by Nazi Germany in 1940. Since the Nazi authorities had initially lenient arrangements which allowed democratic government to remain in power, the Danish Resistance movement was overall slower to develop effective tactics on a large scale, as compared to most other resistance movements. However, the resistance movement did garner effective tactics with time.

The members of the Danish resistance movement engaged in various underground activities such as spying and sabotage. Some essential groups within the resistance movement were the communist BOPA and Holger Danske, both based in Copenhagen. Smaller groups, such as the Samsing Group and the Churchill Group, also played an essential role in contributing to the sabotage efforts.

Dutch Resistance

The Dutch Resistance was in response to the occupation of the Netherlands by Nazi Germany and was mostly non-violent in nature. Most members included those from the Communist Party, churches, and independent groups.

The groups engaged in sabotage and espionage and sheltered downed Allied pilots. Moreover, The Dutch Resistance was also instrumental in protecting and hiding Jewish citizens from the Nazi's forces, as they helped them avoid deportation to concentration camps. Many Dutch individuals and families risked their lives to save Jewish citizens.

Yugoslav Partisans

The Yugoslav Partisans were primarily a communist-led resistance movement based in Yugoslavia which fought against the Axis forces, particularly the Nazis. The movement was successful in liberating Yugoslavia from Axis forces.

The movement was established in 1941 under the leadership of Josip Broz Tito, who eventually became the leader of Yugoslavia. The resistance initially started as a group of guerilla fighters, eventually growing in size and influence. Their primary goal was to liberate Yugoslavia from the Axis forces and establish a unified, socialist state following the war.

The Yugoslav Partisans used a variety of guerilla warfare tactics to intimidate and weaken the Axis opponents: these included ambushes, sabotage, and hit-and-run operations, amongst others. Moreover, they engaged in operations to liberate prisoners of war. The Yugoslavian Partisans as a group were comprised of individuals from multiple ethnicities, including Serbs, Croats, Bosniaks, Slovenians, and Macedonians.

6

ESPIONAGE AND INTELLIGENCE

A nother important aspect of World War 2 was the role of espionage and intelligence gathering during the war. In this chapter, we will discuss the role of codebreakers such as Alan Turing and the work of spy networks such as the OSS and the Abwehr.

USA's Office of Strategic Services (OSS)

The first organization that typically comes to mind when contemplating secret service or intelligence agencies is the U.S. Central Intelligence Agency (CIA), established in 1947. However, during the Second World War, the primary intelligence agency in the United States was the Office of Strategic Services (OSS), serving as the predecessor to the CIA.

Initially created as an agency of the Joint Chiefs of Staff (JCS), the OSS had the mandate to conduct espionage activities on behalf of all branches of the U.S. Armed Forces. Its scope of operations extended beyond espionage to encompass subversion, propaganda, and post-war planning. Before establishing the OSS, the U.S. Army and the U.S. Navy operated separate codebreaking departments: the Signal Intelligence Services and the OP-20-G. The OSS played a pivotal role in consolidating and coordinating these diverse operations under a unified umbrella.

Webwehr

In German, the term "Webwehr" refers to military counterintelligence. From 1920 to 1945, the German military intelligence agency provided services to the Reichswehr and the Wehrmacht. Initially tasked with defending against foreign espionage, the Abwehr underwent significant transformations.

General Kurt von Schleicher played a prominent role in overseeing the Reichswehr from 1926 onwards. Under his leadership, the intelligence units of individual military services were amalgamated. In 1929, these units were centralized under Schleicher's Ministeramt within the Ministry of Defence. This marked the foundational stage of the Abwehr as it is more commonly known.

Admiral Canaris later led the Abwehr to expansion and notable efficiency in the early years of the war. Operation Nordpol, a significant success, targeted the Dutch underground network, supported at the time by the Special Operations Executive. During the Phoney War, the Abwehr focused on collecting information about Denmark and Norway. Surveillance of shipping in and out of Danish and Norwegian ports resulted in the destruction of over 150,000 tons of shipping. Agents in Norway and Denmark successfully infiltrated their military, providing critical insights into the disposition and strength of land forces. Deep-cover Abwehr operatives played a pivotal role in keeping the German forces, especially the Luftwaffe, well-informed during the invasion of Norway. In essence, the Abwehr executed a successful large-scale intelligence operation against both nations, proving indispensable to the success of German military endeavors in the region.

The British Special Operations Executive

Established on 22 July 1940 under the helm of Minister of Economic Warfare Hugh Dalton, the Special Operations Executive (SOE) stands as a clandestine British organization from World War 2. This covert entity resulted from amalgamating three pre-existing secret organizations, operating to conduct espionage, sabotage, and surveillance in occupied Europe. As the conflict progressed, its scope expanded to include occupied Southeast Asia, targeting the Axis powers and supporting local resistance movements.

SOE remained shrouded in secrecy, with only a select few privy to its operations. Those affiliated with or connected to it were colloquially known as the "Baker Street Irregulars," a reference to the location of its London headquarters. Alternately recognized as "Churchill's Secret Army" or the "Ministry of Ungentlemanly Warfare," the organization, and at times its various branches, adopted covert names like the "Joint Technical Board" or the "Inter-Service Research Bureau." Fictitious branches under the Air Ministry, Admiralty, or War Office were also used for added security.

SOE conducted operations in all territories occupied or attacked by Axis forces, except in areas where demarcation lines were established with Britain's principal Allies—the United States and the Soviet Union. SOE occasionally played a pivotal role in utilizing neutral territory and making contingency plans in case neutral countries faced Axis attacks. With a workforce exceeding 13,000 individuals, including approximately 3,200 women, the organization directly employed or controlled a significant number of operatives during its covert operations.

Operation Mincemeat: British Deception Plan

Operation Mincemeat was a successful British deception during the Second World War, concealing the 1943 Allied invasion of Sicily. British intelligence operatives secured the body of Glyndwr Michael, a deceased tramp poisoned by eating rat poison. Transforming him into a Royal Marines officer named Captain (Acting Major) William Martin, they adorned him with personal items indicating his fictional identity. The body also carried correspondence between two British generals, suggesting plans to invade Greece and Sardinia, portraying Sicily as a mere feint.

Integral to the broader Operation Barclay, Mincemeat drew inspiration from the 1939 Trout memo by Rear Admiral John Godfrey and Lieutenant Commander Ian Fleming (Paksoy, 2017). With endorsement from British Prime Minister Winston Churchill and Mediterranean military commander General Dwight D. Eisenhower, the plan unfolded by transporting the body via submarine to the southern coast of Spain. The body was released near the shore and was retrieved by a Spanish fisherman the following morning. The ostensibly neutral Spanish government shared copies of the documents with the German Abwehr intelligence before returning the originals to the British. Forensic analysis confirmed German exposure, as Ultra decrypts revealed their acceptance of the deception. German forces redirected reinforcements to Greece and Sardinia, leaving Sicily vulnerable.

The complete impact of Operation Mincemeat remains uncertain, but Sicily experienced a faster liberation than expected, with lower losses than anticipated.

The Cambridge Five

The Cambridge Five, a covert espionage ring in the United Kingdom, operated from the 1930s through at least the early 1950s, passing vital information to the Soviet Union during the Second World War and the Cold War. Despite their significant activities, none of the known members faced prosecution for their espionage. The gradual revelation of the number and identity of the ring members began in the 1950s.

The public first became aware of the conspiracy in 1951 when Donald Maclean (codenamed Homer) and Guy Burgess (codenamed Hicks) abruptly fled to the Soviet Union. Immediate suspicion fell on Kim Philby (codenamed Sonny, Stanley), who ultimately defected to the Soviet Union in 1963. Following Philby's defection, Anthony Blunt (codenamed Johnson) and John Cairncross (codenamed Liszt) confessed to British intelligence. Blunt's involvement was concealed until 1979, and Cairncross's until 1990, transforming the initial label of the "Cambridge Four" to the "Cambridge Five."

Recruited by the NKVD during their time at the University of Cambridge in the 1930s, the exact timing of their recruitment remains debated. Blunt, a Fellow of Trinity College, was older than Burgess, Maclean, and Philby, serving as a talent spotter and recruiter.

Unified by believing in the superiority of Soviet communism's Marxism-Leninism as a political system and a defense against fascism, all five pursued successful careers within various branches of the British government. Their contributions to Soviet intelligence were substantial, leading the KGB to become suspicious of the authenticity of some information. The gradual unmasking of the Cambridge Five had profound effects on the British establishment, causing demoralization and fostering mistrust in British security, particularly in the United States.

Nazi Operation Bernhard: Counterfeit Notes

Nazi Germany executed Operation Bernhard during World War 2 to forge British banknotes. Initially intended to destabilize the British economy by dropping counterfeit notes over Britain, the project, codenamed Unternehmen Andreas, began in early 1940 under the Sicherheitsdienst (SD). The unit successfully duplicated British rag paper and engraving blocks and deciphered the alpha-numeric serial code. However, internal conflicts led to the project's closure in 1942.

The project was revived later that year with a new goal of financing German intelligence operations, and the operation enlisted prisoners from concentration camps. Led by SS Major Bernhard Krüger at Sachsenhausen concentration camp, the unit produced counterfeit British notes until mid-1945, with estimates ranging from £132.6 million to £300 million. They also advanced their expertise to forge U.S. dollars. The counterfeit currency was laundered for funds and assets. Notably, Operation Bernhard funds were used to pay Elyesa Bazna, codenamed Cicero, for acquiring British secrets. Additionally, £100,000 from the operation facilitated information to free Italian leader Benito Mussolini in the Gran Sasso raid of September 1943.

In early 1945, the unit was moved to the Mauthausen-Gusen concentration camp, then to Redl-Zipf tunnels, and finally to the Ebensee concentration camp. Due to a precise interpretation of a German order, the prisoners were not executed but were liberated by the American Army. Although much of the unit's output was dumped into lakes by the end of the war, sufficient counterfeit money circulated, prompting the Bank of England to halt new note releases and introduce a redesigned currency post-war.

The Enigma Machine

The Enigma Machine is a cipher device that was developed by Nazi Germany and used extensively throughout the war. It was a secure means to encipher secret messages, with an electromechanical rotor mechanism that scrambles the 26 letters of the alphabet. However, although the Enigma Machine allowed Germans to encode their messages and make it extremely difficult to decipher, the British at Bletchley Park and the United States at Arlington Hall successfully broke the Enigma code. Alan Turing, a British mathematician and computer scientist, played a vital role in this effort.

Bletchley Park

Located in England, Bletchley Park was the center for British code-breaking operations. It housed the Government Code and Cypher School, which regularly penetrated the secret communications of the Axis Powers – most importantly, the German Enigma Machine and the Lorenz ciphers. The GC&CS team of codebreakers included Alan Turing, Gordon Welchman, Hugh Alexander, Bill Tutte, and Stuart Milner-Barry. The nature of the work at Bletchley remained secret until many years after the war.

Code Talkers

A code talker was an individual employed by the military during wartime to employ a little-known language for secret communication. Most commonly associated with U.S. service members in the World Wars, these individuals, particularly within the U.S.

Marine Corps, leveraged Native American languages to transmit coded messages, totaling around 400 to 500 personnel.

Code talkers enhanced communication encryption and decryption speed on the front lines, contributing to decisive victories in World War 2, as their codes remained unbroken. Two code types were utilized. One type was a formal development based on languages like Comanche and Navajo, using native words for each English alphabet letter. The other was informal translation directly from English into Indigenous languages, employing short, descriptive phrases if no direct translation existed.

The term "Code Talker" was initially coined by the U.S. Marine Corps, designating individuals who completed specialized training. Today, it remains strongly linked to bilingual Navajo speakers trained in the Navajo Code during World War 2. However, Native American communicators, including the Cherokee, Choctaw, and Lakota, had served in this role during World War 1. The contemporary use of the term "Code Talker" encompasses military personnel from all Native American communities contributing language skills in service to the United States.

Double Agents e.g. Juan Pujol Garcia "Garbo" and D-Day Invasion Plans

In counterintelligence, a double agent is an operative of one country's secret intelligence service who spies on a target organization of another country while concurrently betraying their own organization. During World War 2, Juan Pujol Garcia emerged as a notable double agent, operating as a Spanish spy loyal to Great Britain against Nazi Germany. Codenamed "Garbo" by the British and "Alaric" by the Germans, Pujol created a non-existent spy network called "Arabal."

Motivated by a disdain for political extremism after the Spanish Civil War, Pujol sought to work for the greater good and approached the British Embassy in Madrid, initially facing rejection. Undeterred, he assumed a false identity as a pro-Nazi Spanish official, becoming a German agent. Instead of recruiting agents in Britain as instructed, he moved to Lisbon, crafting fictional reports using diverse public sources.

While the accuracy of his information was questionable, Pujol gained the trust of the Germans by inventing fictitious sub-agents to attribute false information and errors. Recognizing his value, the Allies accepted Pujol when the Germans expended resources, hunting down an imaginary convoy. Pujol codenamed "Garbo," and his handler Tomás Harris expanded the fictitious network throughout the war, communicating with German handlers via letters and later radio. The Germans unwittingly funded a network of 27 entirely fictional agents.

Crucially, Pujol played an essential role in Operation Fortitude, deceiving the Germans about the D-Day invasion in Normandy (Barbier, 1998). His false information convinced the Germans that the main attack would occur in the Pas de Calais, leading them to deploy and maintain significant forces there. Remarkably, Pujol received military honors from both sides, being awarded the Iron Cross by the Germans and becoming a Member of the Order of the British Empire.

7

WOMEN IN WAR

The lead-up to the Second World War witnessed the continuation and further development of feminist movements that had gained momentum during the late 19th and early 20th centuries. The aftermath of World War 1 saw women achieving significant milestones in the fight for suffrage. The war had challenged traditional gender roles, and women's contributions to the war effort were recognized. In the post-war period, many countries granted women the right to vote, including the United States (1920), the United Kingdom, and several European nations. The 1920s and 1930s brought about broader societal changes, challenging traditional gender norms. Women across Western societies began to pursue education and careers, meaning their status was no longer limited to the domestic sphere alone. The concept of the "New Woman" emerged, symbolizing a shift in societal expectations regarding women's roles. Women increasingly entered the workforce during the interwar period, especially during times of economic hardships such as the Great Depression. Although their contributions were often undervalued and underpaid, women's economic independence and participation in various industries expanded.

The outbreak of the Second World War brought about a further transformation in women's roles and status, which echoed but surpassed the changes observed during World War 1. Further in this chapter, we outline some of the ways women played a crucial and multifaceted role, serving as indispensable assets during the war. This change encompasses not only assuming roles traditionally held by men but also engaging in professions such as nursing, which portrays the diverse contributions of women throughout this historical period.

Women in Espionage and Resistance Movements

World War 2 brought an unprecedented demand for personnel, leading to new opportunities for women. The U.S. military established separate branches for women, marking a historical shift. Simultaneously, the war opened avenues for women to participate formally in espionage, a domain traditionally reserved for men.

England took the lead in creating the Special Operations Executive (SOE) in 1940, where women played a significant role as spies, particularly in France, working as couriers and wireless operators. Recognizing this success, the United States established the Office of Strategic Services (OSS) in 1942, its first independent intelligence agency. Building on the SOE's model, the OSS discreetly recruited women to handle top-secret transmissions and engage in classified intelligence work. Elite female agents were sent overseas, many trained at SOE intelligence schools.

Julia McWilliams, a notable OSS employee, rose from secretary to senior intelligence officer. Her overseas assignment in Ceylon led to a fateful encounter with fellow agent Paul Child, whom she later married. Julia gained international fame as a chef post-war.

Beyond official espionage roles, women worldwide joined resistance movements, undertaking covert operations like spying, transporting weapons, aiding escapes, and contributing significantly to the

Allies' success. Their pivotal role extended beyond official channels, showcasing the vital contribution of women during World War 2.

Women in the Work

During the Second World War, women played an essential role in the workforce, marking a significant departure from previous norms and their stereotypical domestic roles. By engaging in various diverse occupations, they could contribute substantially to the war efforts, as they were particularly vital resources in munitions factories, shipbuilding, and aviation. Moreover, women also took on crucial roles in auxiliary services, serving as air-raid wardens, fire officers, evacuation officers, and drivers of fire engines, trains, and trams. The war period also witnessed a shift in some trade unions, traditionally associated with male occupations like engineering, as they began admitting more female members.

Given the entry of women into occupations that were deemed highly skilled and traditionally male, such as drivers of fire engines and roles in the engineering, metal, and shipbuilding industries, discussions about equal pay arose. These debates reflected the changing landscape of women's contributions to the wartime economy and were fruitful in eventually leading to legislation that provided women with greater rights.

The impact of women's empowerment extended beyond factory work, with over six million women taking on wartime jobs, three million volunteering with the Red Cross, and more than 200,000 serving in various military capacities. There were several Women's auxiliary branches established for every branch of the U.S. military, which included the Women's Army Corps (WAC), Women Accepted for Volunteer Emergency Service (WAVES), and Women Airforce Service Pilots (WASP). While women were restricted from combat zones, many preferred to become nurses and provide essential support to injured servicemen. The iconic image of female patriotism, symbolized by Rosie the Riveter, represented only one facet of women's multifaceted contributions to the war effort.

Military Service: Women's Army Corps (WAC) in 1942

The establishment of the Women's Army Corps (WAC) in the United States during World War 2 was a watershed moment that allowed women to serve in noncombat roles and break the tradition where, apart from nurses, women were not considered a part of the U.S. Army. With the creation of the WAC, more than 150,000 women now had the opportunity to contribute directly to the military. Initially designated as the Women's Auxiliary Army Corps (WAAC), WAC members held an official status and received a salary, albeit with relatively limited benefits and salary compared to their male counterparts. In July 1943, following the enlistment of numerous women, the U.S. Army removed the "auxiliary" label, providing full U.S. Army benefits to Women's Army Corps members. In 1980, sixteen thousand women who had initially joined the WAAC were finally granted benefits ordinarily provided to veterans.

Initially, there was a public resistance to women serving in the army. Oveta Culp Hobby, the unit's commander, played an important role in dispelling doubts by highlighting that every woman who served in the military could "release a man for combat" (Bryant, 2016). As a result, women assumed various roles, as they took over clerical assignments and engaged in nontraditional jobs like radio operators, electricians, and air traffic controllers. These WAC members served with distinction worldwide, including North Africa, Europe, and Asia during the war.

Night Witches

Women also played a significant role in the military in the case of the Soviet Union during the war. In this context, the "Night Witches" served as a German moniker for the exclusively female aviators from the 588th Night Bomber Regiment. They were later recognized as the 46th "Taman" Guards Night Bomber Aviation Regiment within the Soviet Air Forces. Despite the official prohibition of women from combat roles, Major Marina Raskova utilized her position and personal ties with Soviet leader Joseph Stalin to establish female combat units. The decision to incorporate women into combat roles was driven by practical necessity rather than a quest for gender equality.

On October 8, 1941, an order was issued to deploy three women's airforce units, including the 588th Regiment. Founded by Raskova and spearheaded by Major Yevdokiya Bershanskaya, this regiment predominantly comprised female volunteers in their late teens and early twenties. Operational from 1942 until the war's conclusion in 1945, the regiment executed harassment and precision bombing missions against the Nazi German military. At its zenith, the unit comprised 40 two-person crews, completing over 23,000 sorties and dropping over 3,000 tons of bombs and 26,000 incendiary shells. As the most highly decorated female unit in the Soviet Air Force, several pilots undertook over 800 missions, with twenty-three earning the Hero of the Soviet Union title. Tragically, thirty-two members lost their lives during the war.

Using Polikarpov U-2 biplanes and wooden-and-canvas aircraft initially designed for training and crop dusting, the regiment showcased effectiveness despite their dated origins (1928). The U-2LNB version proved efficient in the night harassment attack missions carried out by the 588th Regiment.

Nursing and Medical Roles

The Second World War placed nurses in unprecedented proximity to the front lines of the war, allowing them to showcase their skills in extreme and perilous conditions across various war zones. Despite the heightened risk of becoming prisoners of war, the value of their service and the lives they saved outweighed the inherent dangers.

The Army Nurse Corps, the oldest among the Federal Nursing Services, was established shortly after the Spanish-American War. While only 1,000 nurses were on their rolls before the attack on Pearl Harbor, this number surged to 12,000 in the later years of the war. Over 59,000 American nurses served in the Army Nurse Corps during World War 2, substantially contributing to the war efforts. They served in field hospitals, evacuation hospitals, hospital trains, hospital ships, and as flight nurses on medical transport planes. Their skill and dedication played a significant role, drastically reducing the death rate among American soldiers who received medical care in the field to less than 4 percent.

Propaganda and Support Roles: e.g., American Women's Voluntary Services

In addition to assuming roles traditionally held by men and making significant contributions to the medical field, women also played vital support roles during World War 2. The American Women's Voluntary Services (AWVS) emerged as the largest women's service organization in the United States during this period, mobilizing women volunteers for various support services to bolster the country's war effort. These services encompassed message delivery, ambulance driving, war bond sales, emergency kitchens, cycle corps driving, dog-sled team operation, aircraft spotting, navigation, aerial photography, firefighting, truck driving, and canteen work. Some of AWVS's responsibilities overlapped with those of the Office of Civilian Defense and the American Red Cross.

Established by Alice Throckmorton McLean in January 1940, 23 months before the United States entered the war, AWVS took inspiration from the British Women's Voluntary Services preparing the country for war. Despite its founders being predominantly wealthy internationalist women and the organization's headquarters being in New York City, suspicions arose among America's isolationists. The AWVS faced challenges, with some viewing it as alarmist and others resisting the idea of women engaging in such activities. Despite these concerns, the AWVS boasted approximately 18,000 members by the time of the attack on Pearl Harbor on December 7, 1941.

How women's role in WWII laid the foundation for gender equity and equality in the preceding years.

During the war, women demonstrated their ability to excel in roles that were traditionally held by men. As men enlisted for the war and the demand for war materials increased, job opportunities in manufacturing opened up for women, offering them greater opportunities and improved salaries. Before the war, most women served as homemakers, with those employed outside the home typically working as secretaries or store clerks.

As millions of men went off to war, women stepped into both civilian and military roles they left behind. Proudly serving their country, their wartime contributions sparked reflections on changing societal views of men and women. The government used posters and films portraying glamorous women in the workplace to encourage female participation in the workforce. The iconic image of Rosie the Riveter, featuring a confident woman in coveralls and a red bandana flexing her muscles with the caption "We Can Do It!" became a powerful symbol of World War 2. Intended to inspire patriotism, Rosie the Riveter represented a new way of portraying women and served as an inspiration for female liberation, according to many historians. Initially considered a temporary measure, the call for women to join the workforce during the war led to the expectation that they would leave these jobs afterward. Some women were content with this arrangement, but those who remained gained new skills and increased confidence. Unfortunately, women who continued to work often faced demotions.

Despite slow progress in the subsequent decades, women's experiences during World War 2 empowered them to challenge traditional gender roles. They fought for the right to work in different jobs, receive equal pay, and have broader rights in the workplace and society.

8

MILITARY TACTICS AND STRATEGY, WEAPONRY AND TECHNOLOGY

B oth the Allied and Axis powers employed several different military strategies and tactics during the Second World War. In this chapter, we will discuss a number of these strategies and tactics, ranging from the German Blitzkrieg and Island Hopping in the Pacific to the Soviet Scorched Earth Policy and Strategic Retreats.

Island Hopping

An important military strategy during the Second World War was island hopping, employed mainly by the United States in the Pacific Theatre. Instead of occupying all the Japanese islands by force, the United States opted to target strategically located islands to use them as airfields and bases to advance further attacks. This strategy was an essential tool for the Allies to push back Japanese forces in the Pacific.

Guerilla Warfare

Guerilla Warfare was another crucial aspect of the war, used extensively worldwide. Guerilla warfare may be viewed as synchronous to the resistance movements against occupying forces and Nazi-collaborationist governments around the globe, in particular Europe. As we have discussed in our earlier chapters, several European countries occupied by Hitler's forces saw the emergence of resistance movements meant to serve as a resistance to the occupying forces. However, these movements were not limited to serving resistance to German forces alone, as they were also often seen against other Axis forces such as Italy and Japan. Besides, partisan warfare was also common in countries like France, Italy, Yugoslavia, and Greece, where local resistance groups engaged in guerilla tactics such as ambushes, sabotage, and hit-and-run attacks against the Axis supply lines and communication networks. Guerilla warfare was also evident on the Eastern Front, where Soviet Partisans disrupted supply lines and attacked German military installations and personnel. Some of the Soviet guerilla groups also made use of scorched earth tactics to destroy the enemy's infrastructure and resources that were vital to their use. On the Asian front, guerilla warfare was crucial in the Chinese resistance against Japanese occupation. Chinese forces often operated under challenging terrains, seeking to disrupt Japanese supply lines and resources. Similarly, Filipino Guerrilla groups also played an essential role in resisting Japanese occupation, as they would carry out sabotage missions, collect intelligence, and support Allied forces during the later stages of their campaign in the Pacific region.

Trench Warfare

Another significant military strategy that stood out during the Second World War was Trench Warfare. Militaries dug up trenches as a defense tactic across the Eastern Front during the Siege Warfare, the Italian Campaign, and the Pacific Islands. However, this strategy was less prevalent than during the First World War. In the Pacific Theatre in particular, during the island-hopping campaigns, there were instances where Japanese forces dug in and created numerous extensive defensive positions. On islands such as Iwo Jima and Okinawa, the Japanese defenders constructed a vast network of tunnels, bunkers, and fortified positions, which was akin to trench warfare. At the Italian front, both the Allies and the Axis powers engaged in trench-like warfare in battles like the Battle of Monte Cassino.

Strategic Bombing

The Second World War saw a relentless push towards strategic bombing, which involved targeting railways, harbors, cities, civilian homes, and industrial areas in enemy territories. Strategic bombing was distinct from the close air support provided to ground forces and tactical air power. Instead, it aimed to weaken the enemy's industrial and political backbone, which served as a departure from the focus being purely on military targets.

The strategic bombing saga began on September 1, 1939, with Germany's invasion of Poland, marked by the Luftwaffe launching aerial bombardments of Polish cities and civilians. As the war unfolded, both the Axis and the Allies significantly intensified their bombing campaigns. For instance, the Royal Air Force retaliated to Luftwaffe attacks on the United Kingdom in October 1939 by targeting military installations in Germany. The Blitz, initiated by the

Luftwaffe in September 1940, specifically targeted British civilians. The bombing focus shifted to Soviet cities and infrastructure with the onset of Operation Barbarossa in June 1941. The British, starting in February 1942, broadened their bombing campaign against Germany to include industrial sites and civilian areas. On the other hand, the United States further strengthened these efforts upon entering the war, engaging in controversial firebombings in cities like Hamburg (1943) and Dresden (1945).

On the Pacific front, the Japanese frequently targeted civilian populations, as evident in the case of bombings of cities like Chongqing. U.S. air raids on Japan reached a climax in October 1944, culminating in widespread firebombing and the final atomic bombings of Hiroshima and Nagasaki in August 1945.

The effectiveness of these strategic bombing campaigns remains a subject of debate. Although they did not single-handedly secure decisive military victories, some argue that targeting non-military sites significantly weakened enemy industrial capabilities, a viewpoint supported by Japan's surrender. The human cost, with estimates ranging from hundreds of thousands to over a million deaths, resulted in the mass displacement of civilians and extensive destruction of major cities, particularly in Europe and Asia.

The Blitz

The Blitzkrieg, or "lightning war," was a strategic bombing campaign by the German Army, primarily against the United Kingdom from 1940 to 1941. This offensive method of warfare involved the striking of swift, focused blows on the opponent's army using mobile, maneuverable forces that included armored tanks and air support. Such attacks typically led to a quick victory, limiting the losses to the soldiers and the artillery. Historically, Blitzkrieg was rooted in an earlier military strategy proposed by the Prussian general Carl von Clausewitz in the 19th century (Hughes, 2020). He had proposed the "concentration principle", according to which making a single decisive blow against a specific target (the "Schwerpunkt" or center of gravity) was more effective than dispersing those forces. The outcomes of the First World War made the German leaders realize that the overall lack of mobilized, maneuverable forces and flexible tactics had caused the conflicts to become deadly wars of attrition.

The Blitzkrieg strategy, which aimed to target critical industrial areas, ports, and urban centers belonging to the Allied forces, was adopted by the German Luftwaffe. It sought to disrupt the production capabilities, weaken transportation networks, and instill fear among the locals. The strategy adopted several tactics associated with Blitzkrieg in the Spanish Civil War in 1939 and the invasion of Poland in 1939, including Panzer tank divisions to quickly defeat the poorly equipped Polish troops.

This use of the Blitzkrieg strategy came to the limelight in May 1940 when Germany invaded Belgium, the Netherlands, and France. During this time, the German army used the collective force of tanks, artillery troops, and mobile infantry to drive through the Ardennes Forest and quickly penetrate the Allied defenses. With the close support and coordination by the Luftwaffe (German air force) and the advantage of radio communication to assist in coordinating military strategy, the Germans could march through the Northern French territories towards the English Channel. They were able to bomb London, among other British cities, pushing the British Expeditionary Force into a pocket near Dunkirk. Already undergoing fragmentation, by the end of June 1940, the French Army had collapsed. Moreover, the German Army had also used the Blitzkrieg tactic against the Soviet Army during their invasion of the Soviet Union. Although they had expected a short campaign, similar to the one encountered in Western Europe the previous spring, the strategy proved less successful since the Soviet army was more organized and well-armed.

Towards the end of the Second World War, the Allies had effectively incorporated Blitzkrieg strategies to their advantage, particularly during critical conflicts such as the European operations and the Battle of Stalingrad commanded by U.S. General George Patton in 1944. General Patton had led the U.S. army in the Mediterranean Theatre of the war, and during this time, he had meticulously analyzed the German campaigns in Poland and France. Following this stint, he advocated for swift and decisive actions to mitigate the risk of protracted and resource-intensive conflicts.

Radar Technology

Radar technology emerged as a crucial factor during the Second World War, with both the Allies and Axis harnessing the power of this innovative radio-based detection and tracking system. The fundamental principle of the technology involved transmitting radio waves to detect distant objects, measuring the time it took for the resulting 'echo' produced upon striking an object to reflect back to the receiver. This method not only facilitated the detection of objects at a distance but also enabled the identification of their height and bearing, including the direction of flight for aerial targets.

At the onset of the Second World War in 1939, a network of early warning radar stations, known as Chain Home (CH) stations, had already been established along the southern and eastern coasts of Britain. The CH stations were monumental static installations that featured steel transmitter masts exceeding 100 meters in height and played an essential role in the Battle of Britain. Radar technology demonstrated its capability to detect incoming enemy aircraft at a range of 80 miles, providing crucial early warnings to the British air defenses.

Despite the effectiveness of the CH stations, a significant breakthrough took place in 1940 with the introduction of the cavity magnetron. This innovation brought the world into a new era, producing more potent radio waves with a shorter wavelength. Consequently, this technological advancement enabled the development of radar units that were more compact, powerful, and sensitive. The Allies swiftly capitalized on this breakthrough, gaining a substantial technological edge over the radar designs employed by the Axis forces. This progress led to the rapid development of new radar equipment for deployment in aircraft, ships, and land warfare, which significantly enhanced the overall capabilities of the Allied forces.

Night Bombing

Following the First World War, nations extensively invested in enhancing their strategic and defensive capabilities, focusing on air power. By the mid-1930s, a shift in perspectives regarding aircraft occurred, emphasizing the concept of daylight raids conducted by modern fighter jets. Many countries endeavored to retrofit existing aircraft with the necessary tools and technology to conduct nighttime aerial raids.

The Luftwaffe, for instance, employed radar technology in their aircraft to execute nighttime raids on British cities. Single-engined aircraft, such as the Arado Ar 68 and early Messerschmitt Bf 109 models, were adapted for the night-fighter role. These aircraft, colloquially known as "Wilde Sau" or wild boar, were equipped with a direction finder and landing lights for navigation in the dark.

To locate targets, accompanying aircraft, guided from the ground, dropped strings of flares in front of the bombers. Alternatively, the illumination from burning cities provided sufficient light for target identification.

In contrast, the U.S. Army Air Forces focused on daytime bombing over Germany and Axis allies, proving statistically more effective than nighttime raids. British night-bombing attacks exhibited a success rate of only one of 100 targets successfully hit. Responding to British requests and seeking to sell aircraft to the Allies, the U.S. adapted day fighters to a night role, including the Douglas P-70 and later the Lockheed P-38M "Night Lightning". Although the purpose-built night fighter Northrop P-61 Black Widow was introduced, its deployment was limited, and the British had ample supplies of their own designs. Simultaneously, the U.S. Navy initiated Project Affirm in 1942 to develop night fighting equipment and tactics. Urgency arose after successful Japanese nighttime harassment in the Solomon Islands. VF(N)-75 became the first U.S. Navy night fighter squadron in April 1943, with carrier-launched fighter combat missions starting in January 1944. Additionally, equipped with radar sets, planes like the Grumman F6F Hellcat and Vought F4U Corsair played a crucial role in countering kamikaze attacks during the Battle of Leyte Gulf.

Carpet Bombing

Carpet bombing, also referred to as saturation bombing, was an essential military strategy used by both the Allied and the Axis powers. Carpet bombing involves a comprehensive bombardment of a selected land area to cause damage across its entirety. The term causes an image of explosions covering the area, similar to how a carpet covers a floor.

In the inter-war years, there was a growing anticipation that cities would have to undergo swift destruction as a result of bombing raids upon the outbreak of war. This expectation was based upon the anticipated use of poison gas and substantial devastation caused by high-explosive bombs. The trend was set in motion with the aerial bombardment of Warsaw on September 25, 1939, during the opening stages of the conflict. The Rotterdam Blitz in May 1940 further exemplified this approach, causing extensive destruction and compelling the Dutch to surrender. Initially, the RAF Bomber Command lacked the prerequisite navigation systems and amount of bombers to conduct large-scale attacks in Nazi Germany. As heavy bombers and technological advancements came into play, the focus shifted to target civilian populations working in war-related industries, which marked a departure from the earlier intention to avoid collateral damage.

The Eighth Air Force of the USAAF arrived in Britain in 1942, supporting the Soviet Union with a bombing campaign, as there was reluctance to open a new front in Europe. The firebombing of Hamburg and subsequent attacks on cities like Dresden displayed this strategy, causing significant damage to industrial worker accommodations. Carpet bombing was employed not only as part of strategic bombing but also as close air support for ground operations, often known as "flying artillery." This tactic, exemplified by Sir Arthur Tedder's bomb-carpet in the Tunisia Campaign, continued during the Normandy Campaign and the Pacific War.

During the Pacific War, carpet bombing was used as a strategy to extensively target Japanese cities, with the March 1945 Tokyo bombing causing devastating casualties and leaving countless people homeless. Similarly, carpet bombing attacks on the Japanese cities of Kobe, Osaka, and Nagoya further contributed to the large-scale destruction. By the time of the atomic bombings on Hiroshima and Nagasaki, many urban areas had already been reduced to rubble.

In the Philippines, carpet bombing was used against Japanese forces in Manila and Baguio during the war's final months, resulting in the near-total destruction of these cities. In particular, Manila (Philippines) became the second-most-destroyed city of World War 2.

The Enola Gay and the Atomic Bomb

The B-29, also known as the Superfortress, was a four-engine heavy bomber manufactured by Boeing. It was introduced in 1942 and gained prominence in the Pacific Theater during the Second World War. In 1944, the B-29 was chosen to carry the atomic bomb, leading to modifications, including reinforcements of the bomb bay. Lieutenant Colonel Tibbets, an experienced B-29 pilot, assembled and trained a crew. The modified B-29s were subsequently flown to the U.S. military base on Tinian in the Mariana Islands.

On July 16, 1945, the United States successfully tested an atomic bomb during the Trinity test. President Harry S. Truman informed of this development during the Potsdam Conference. He conveyed to Soviet leader Joseph Stalin that the United States now possessed "a new weapon of unusual destructive force" (Gooderson, 2008). On July 26, the Allied leaders demanded Japan's unconditional surrender or else face "prompt and utter destruction." With Japan's refusal, the United States decided to deploy an atomic bomb on Hiroshima, Japan, on August 6, 1945, destroying approximately three-quarters of the city. The atomic bomb was codenamed "Little Boy". Subsequently, on August 9, 1945, a second atomic bomb, codenamed "Fat Man," was dropped on Nagasaki, influencing Japan's surrender decision.

Messerschmitt Bf 109

The Messerschmitt Bf 109, a German World War 2 fighter aircraft and a vital component of the Luftwaffe's fighter force alongside the Focke-Wulf Fw 190, first entered operational service in 1937 during the Spanish Civil War. Its service continued until the end of World War 2 in 1945. Recognized for its advanced features, including all-metal monocoque construction, retractable landing gear, and a closed canopy, the Bf 109 was powered by a liquid-cooled, inverted V12 aero engine. Despite being officially designated as such, Allied aircrew and some German aces commonly referred to it as the Me-109.

The Bf-109 was conceived as an interceptor and eventually evolved into various roles, serving as a bomber escort, fighter-bomber, day- and night-fighter, all-weather fighter, ground-attack aircraft, and aerial reconnaissance aircraft. Designed by Willy Messerschmitt and Robert Lusser at Bayerische Flugzeugwerke in the early to mid-1930s, the Bf 109 achieved significant production numbers, totaling 34,248 airframes from 1936 to April 1945. Notably, a portion of the production occurred in Nazi concentration camps through forced labor.

Very soon, the Bf-109 earned the distinction of being the most-produced fighter aircraft in history. Remarkably versatile, it served multiple countries beyond World War 2, demonstrating its enduring impact. It played an essential role on the Eastern Front, flown by the top-scoring fighter aces of all time, including Erich Hartmann, who claimed 352 victories. Other notable successes, such as Hans-Joachim Marseille and Ilmari Juutilainen from Finland, also achieved significant success with the Bf 109. Pilots from various countries, including Italy, Romania, Croatia, Bulgaria, and Hungary, further contributed to the aircraft's legacy. Despite continuous development, the Bf 109 remained competitive with the latest Allied fighter aircraft until the war's conclusion.

Spitfire

The Supermarine Spitfire was a British single-seat fighter aircraft the Royal Air Force (RAF) and Allies used during the Second World War. It featured numerous variants, ranging from the Mk 1 to the Rolls-Royce Griffon-engined Mk 24. The Spitfire enjoys ongoing popularity, remaining the sole British fighter in continuous production throughout the war, with around 70 airworthy examples and static exhibits in aviation museums globally.

Initially designed as a short-range, high-performance interceptor by R. J. Mitchell, the chief designer at Supermarine Aviation Works, the Spitfire underwent a crucial design element – its elliptical wing, crafted by Beverley Shenstone. The incorporation of sunken rivets resulted in a thin cross-section, contributing to a top speed that surpassed its contemporaries. Mitchell continued refining the design until he died in 1937. Following Mitchell's passing, Joseph Smith assumed leadership, overseeing subsequent iterations and advancements in the Spitfire's development.

During the Battle of Britain (July–October 1940), the public perception favored the Spitfire, although the Hurricane also played a vital role. The Spitfire was a superior fighter aircraft, demonstrating lower attrition and a higher victory-to-loss ratio and engaging primarily with Luftwaffe fighters, notably the Messerschmitt Bf 109E.

Dive Bombers

The dive bombers were an early military aircraft designed to dive directly at a specific target, release bombs at low altitudes, level off abruptly, and depart. Originating from an experimental Allied sortie in World War 1, post-World War 2 developments such as precision-guided munitions and improved anti-aircraft defenses altered the landscape. New weapons like rockets enhanced accuracy from smaller dive angles and greater distances. During the Battle of Britain and the invasion of Poland and France, the Stuka dive bomber played a vital role, breaking defenses and facilitating strategic advances for the German forces. However, the Stuka's vulnerabilities became apparent when faced with fighter opposition, leading to its withdrawal from operations over the United Kingdom.

The German Stuka, known for its adaptability, underwent modifications such as including autocannons, enabling it to destroy tanks effectively. Notably, Germany's Hans-Ulrich Rudel emerged as the most successful dive-bomber pilot, contributing to the sinking of a Soviet battleship and claiming over 100 Soviet tanks destroyed. The German Ju 87G Kanonenvogel, equipped with powerful cannons, proved to be a lethal weapon against Allied tanks.

The Italian Regia Aeronautica's Breda Ba.65 faced vulnerability against British fighters in the Mediterranean. In retrospect, the American Curtiss P-40 Warhawks deployed in Morocco successfully shot down German Ju 87Ds. The U.S. Army Air Forces also modified North American P-51 Mustangs into dive bombers, proving effective in Africa, Italy, and Asia.

On the other hand, the Royal Navy's Fairey Barracuda replaced torpedo-dive bombers, making successful diving attacks on the German battleship Tirpitz in a Norwegian fjord in 1944. The Soviet Union Armed Forces deployed the Arkhangelsky Ar-2 and the Petlyakov Pe-2, showcasing their use in the evolving landscape of aerial warfare.

Strategic Reconnaissance

Aerial reconnaissance involves utilizing reconnaissance aircraft for military or strategic purposes, serving various needs such as artillery spotting, collecting imagery intelligence, and observing enemy maneuvers. A significant transformation in aerial reconnaissance occurred during 1939–45, particularly in Britain and the United States. This expansion initially relied on trial and error, introducing new tactics, procedures, and technology, often without requiring specialized aircraft types. The mission diversified into sub-types and incorporated different electronic forms of reconnaissance.

In 1928, the Royal Air Force developed an electric heating system for aerial cameras, enabling reconnaissance aircraft to capture images from high altitudes without camera parts freezing. In 1939, RAF's Sidney Cotton and Flying Officer Maurice Longbottom proposed a radical idea of employing fast, smaller aircraft for airborne reconnaissance, leveraging speed and high service ceilings to avoid detection. This innovative thinking led to developing Spitfire PR variants, where armaments were replaced with extra fuel and cameras. With a maximum speed of 396 mph at 30,000 feet, the Spitfire PR became highly successful in photo-reconnaissance missions. Besides, numerous Spitfire variants were subsequently built for this purpose, initially serving with the Photographic Reconnaissance Unit (PRU).

Beyond Spitfires, other fighters like the British Mosquito and the American P-38 Lightning and P-51 Mustang were also adapted for photo-reconnaissance. These aircraft, often painted in PRU Blue or Pink camouflage to blend with the sky, had stripped weapons and modified engines for enhanced performance at high altitudes exceeding 40,000 feet.

Paratroopers

A paratrooper is a military parachutist trained for airborne operations, often involved in surprise attacks to seize strategic objectives like airfields or bridges. The extensive use of military parachutists and parachutes for troop distribution and transportation began during World War 2.

One of the most significant airborne assaults in history occurred during the D-Day Allied invasion of Normandy. Paratroopers from the British 6th Airborne Division, the U.S. 82nd and 101st Airborne Divisions, and the 1st Canadian Parachute Battalion participated in this operation. Over 13,000 paratroopers were flown in approximately 925 C-47 airplanes from southern England to the Cotentin Peninsula. An additional 4,000 men, including glider infantry and supporting units, were scheduled to arrive in 500 gliders afterward on D-Day to reinforce the paratroopers.

The paratroopers faced a challenging night jump behind enemy lines five hours prior to the coastal landings. Despite being badly scattered, with many sustaining injuries and casualties, the paratroopers fought valiantly, causing confusion among the German commanders and keeping their troops occupied. Despite harsh weather, darkness, and disorganization, the resourcefulness of soldiers and leaders ensured that the Utah Beach assault objectives were eventually achieved. Simultaneously, British and Canadian attacks successfully secured the left flank of the invasion force.

Strategic Transportation (e.g., American C-47 Dakota)

Strategic transportation also played a crucial role in World War 2 air power, with significant contributions from the C-47, a versatile

U.S. military transport aircraft. Derived from the successful Douglas DC-3, a twin-engine low-wing monoplane that revolutionized commercial aviation in 1935, the C-47 became an important military asset during the war and continued its service long afterward.

Initially ordered by the Army Air Forces in 1939, the military version of the DC-3, known as the C-53 Skytrooper, entered production in October 1941, with around 250 units produced. The definitive military variant, the C-47, featured a reinforced fuselage, strengthened cabin floors for heavy loads, large rear fuselage doors for cargo loading and paratroop drops, and more powerful engines. Production commenced in January 1942, and over 10,000 C-47s were manufactured until production ceased in the summer of 1945. The C-47 had a wingspan of 95 feet, was powered by two 1,200-horsepower Pratt & Whitney radial engines, had a length of 64 feet, and a crew of three (pilot, copilot, and loadmaster/navigator). With a cruise speed of 155 miles (250 km) per hour and a range of 1,600 miles (2,600 km), it exhibited versatility in various roles. Designated as R4D by the U.S. Navy and Dakota by the British Royal Air Force and other English-speaking forces, the C-47 came in numerous versions. While some served as VIP transports and a few featured sleeping accommodations, most were equipped with metal bench seats accommodating 28 fully armed troops.

The C-47's normal payload capacity was 5,000 pounds (2,300 kg), but in emergencies, it could handle up to 6,000 pounds (2,700 kg) or even 7,000 pounds (3,200 kg). With spacious rear-fuselage cargo doors, the aircraft could transport jeeps, light trucks, or equivalent cargo, allowing for in-flight troops or cargo drops via parachutes. This capability, combined with its generous cabin space, made the C-47 the premier paratroop delivery aircraft of the war. Additionally, the C-47 could pull two CG-4 Waco assault gliders or one larger British Horsa glider. As an aerial ambulance, the C-47 could accommodate 18 stretchers and a medical team of three.

9

PROPAGANDA

"The essence of propaganda consists in winning people over to an idea so sincerely, so vitally, that in the end they succumb to it utterly and can never again escape from it."

Joseph Goebbels wrote this in his diary, and Adolph Hitler agreed. After the Nazis' rise to power in 1933, Hitler set up a Reich Ministry of Public Enlightenment and Propaganda, making Goebbels its chief. Goebbels promoted the Nazi message through art, music, theatre, films, books, radio, and the press while censoring all opposition. Moreover, Goebbels sought to inflame the anger of Germans over their defeat in the First World War and highlight German cultural and military achievements to boost German national pride. As such, he played a significant role in creating an atmosphere in Germany that served as an enabler for the Nazis to commit terrible atrocities against Jews and other minorities. However, as we will discover in this chapter, the use of propaganda was not limited to Nazi Germany alone, as it was also extensively used by Allied countries, in particular the United States.

Nazi Propaganda

In the years following World War 1, Nazi propaganda strategically targeted discrimination against ethnic Germans in eastern European nations. These countries had gained territory at Germany's expense, becoming a focal point for cultivating political loyalty and fostering a heightened "race consciousness" among ethnic German populations. The underlying objective was to present Germany's demands for concessions and annexations as not only justifiable but reasonable in the eyes of foreign governments.

The narrative of Nazi propaganda took a dark turn with the German invasion of the Soviet Union. Emphasizing themes that linked Soviet Communism to European Jewry, Germany was portrayed as the stalwart defender of "Western" culture against the perceived "Judeo-Bolshevik threat." This narrative gained momentum following the catastrophic German defeat at Stalingrad in 1943. Its influence extended beyond Nazi supporters, potentially impacting non-Nazi Germans and local collaborators, fostering a determination to persist in the war effort.

Central to Nazi propaganda was the demonization of the perceived enemies of the Nazi Party, which included not only the Jews but also communists, capitalists, and intellectuals. The propaganda machine tirelessly promoted Nazi values, extolling heroic death, the Führerprinzip (leader principle), Volksgemeinschaft (people's community), Blut und Boden (blood and soil), and a sense of pride in the concept of the Germanic Herrenvolk (master race). The cult of personality surrounding Adolf Hitler was carefully maintained, and campaigns advocating for eugenics and the annexation of German-speaking areas were actively endorsed.

As World War 2 erupted, Nazi propaganda intensified its efforts to vilify Germany's enemies, with particular focus on the United

Kingdom, the Soviet Union, and the United States. By 1943, facing challenges on multiple fronts, Nazi propaganda took a drastic turn, urging the German population to embrace the concept of total war. This change marked a critical moment in the propaganda machinery, as it sought to consolidate support for the war effort and manipulate public perception in the face of escalating global conflicts.

Use of Radio Broadcasts by both Allies and Axis

Among the diverse array of tools wielded by nations on both sides of the conflict, radio broadcasts emerged as a powerful and influential medium for shaping perceptions and mobilizing citizens. As the war unfolded, nations recognized the strategic importance of utilizing radio to disseminate propaganda, influencing their own populations and attempting to sway opinions across enemy lines. The Allies and Axis powers, each attuned to the potential of this mass communication tool, engaged in a battle of words and narratives that played out over the airwaves.

Radio broadcasting was central to disseminating information and shaping public opinion in the United States. With 90% of American families owning a radio during World War 2, it became widespread in households nationwide. However, the challenge lay in navigating the delicate balance between disseminating government-approved information and avoiding the perception of censorship.

President Roosevelt, recognizing the skepticism towards propaganda, adopted a nuanced approach. The "you technique" became a successful method, which immersed the listener in personal situations such as battle scenarios or military camps. This personalized approach aimed to bridge the gap between the government and the public and foster a sense of shared responsibility in the war effort.

Across the Atlantic, in Nazi Germany, radio was harnessed as a potent propaganda tool. German propagandists transmitted close to 11 hours of programming daily, a significant portion of it in English, to erode pro-British sentiments. Specific groups, such as capitalists, Jews, and targeted newspapers, were focal points in the propaganda narrative.

In Britain, radio broadcasts were crucial in bolstering morale and disseminating information. Edward R. Murrow's iconic news reports, vividly detailing the Battle of Britain and nightly bombing raids, captured the imagination of the entire nation and provided a counterpoint to Nazi propaganda.

Films and Newsreels

Movies and films also served as an effective medium for states to further their propaganda. This medium effectively shaped perceptions, boosted morale, and influenced public opinion.

In the United States, Hollywood emerged as a crucial player in producing films that staunchly supported the war effort. These cinematic creations depicted heroic soldiers, patriotic citizens, and the triumph of good over evil. Notable examples such as "Casablanca" and "Mrs. Miniver" conveyed powerful messages of sacrifice and resilience.

On the Axis front, Nazi Germany harnessed the potential of film as a strategic tool for disseminating propaganda. Propaganda Minister Joseph Goebbels maintained tight control over the German film industry, producing movies that glorified the regime, vilified enemies, and promoted the Nazi ideology. Leni Riefenstahl's documentary

"Triumph of the Will" stands out as a prime example of this cinematic propaganda, showcasing the 1934 Nazi Party Congress.

In Japan, films like "The Battle of China" were crafted to bolster nationalistic fervor. The Japanese government exercised strict regulation over the film industry to align with its wartime objectives, emphasizing themes of loyalty, sacrifice, and the righteousness of the imperial cause. This intersection of film and propaganda became a powerful force in shaping the narratives that unfolded on both sides of the global conflict.

Posters and Print Media

Besides films and electronic media, posters and print media also played a crucial role as a method for states to extend their wartime propaganda. The United States, in particular, utilized posters extensively, producing more propaganda posters than any other country involved in World War 2, with almost 200,000 different designs printed during the war. These posters employed various themes to encourage support for the war, covering areas such as conservation, production, recruitment, home efforts, and secrecy.

Strategically placed in areas without paid advertisements, these posters found spaces in post offices, railroad stations, schools, restaurants, and retail stores. Smaller versions adorned the windows of private homes and apartment buildings, reaching audiences where other forms of propaganda media were impractical. The government agency overseeing the production and distribution of propaganda posters was the Office of War Information (OWI) Bureau of Graphics.

Compared to that of Britain and other allies, a notable distinction in U.S. poster propaganda was its predominantly positive messaging. U.S. posters focused on duty, patriotism, and tradition, avoiding the approach of fuelling hatred for the enemy seen in posters from other nations. The positive messages aimed to boost production on the home front, emphasizing duty and patriotism. American posters seldom depicted war casualties, and battlefield scenes gave way to commercial images, meeting the "consumer" demand for war-related content. Notably, the government did not design these posters; artists created them without compensation. Competitions held by government agencies allowed artists to submit their designs, providing a diverse array of options for selection.

Moreover, the United States also used leaflets to convey essential messages and informational tidbits to citizens. This was done by dropping leaflets from airplanes in locations that were otherwise unreachable by other means. Interestingly, an entire squadron of B-17 bombers was used entirely for this purpose.

Censorship

Apart from utilizing information for propaganda, states employed censorship to manage information and mold public perception of their wartime endeavors.

In Germany, the media landscape was tightly controlled by Joseph Goebbels. The Nazi regime censored and manipulated news, films, and publications to conform to its ideological narrative, suppressing information conflicting with Nazi ideology while widely disseminating propaganda supporting the regime's views and demonizing enemies.

Likewise, censorship played a crucial role in information management in the United States and other Allied nations. The objective was to prevent the leakage of sensitive military details that could aid the enemy and to maintain a unified and positive narrative for the public. The U.S. Office of Censorship regulated news, letters, and other forms of communication, ensuring the dissemination of information aligned with national interests.

Censorship also extended to cultural productions such as films, ensuring they conveyed messages supporting the war effort and upheld public morale. Scenes containing sensitive military information or potentially demoralizing content were edited or removed entirely.

Enemy Atrocity Propaganda

Atrocity propaganda involves the dissemination of information about the crimes committed by an enemy, often incorporating deliberate fabrications or exaggerations. This type of propaganda can manifest through various mediums, including photographs, videos, interviews, illustrations, and other forms of information presentation. The inherently violent nature of war frequently leads to the exaggeration and invention of atrocities, becoming a focal point of propaganda. Patriotism alone might not be enough to cultivate hatred toward the enemy. Hence, propaganda served as a necessary tool. Harold Lasswell observes that modern nations' psychological resistance to war mandates framing every war as a defense against a menacing aggressor, leaving no ambiguity about whom the public should disdain.

In World War 2, propaganda films such as "Hitler's Children," "Women in Bondage," and "Enemy of Women" portrayed Germans, extending beyond just Nazis, as enemies of civilization, depicting them as abusers of women and the innocent (Delwiche, 2009). The Germans extensively utilized atrocity propaganda, both preceding and during the war. Episodes of violence between ethnic Germans and Poles, like the 1939 Bloody Sunday massacre, were portrayed as the brutal slaughter of the German population by subhuman Poles, serving as a justification for the genocide of the Polish population outlined in the Nazi General Plan Ost. In the later stages of the war, Nazi propaganda relied on exaggerated depictions of actual or planned Allied actions against Germany, such as the bombing of Dresden, the Nemmersdorf massacre, and the Morgenthau Plan for the deindustrialization of Germany, to instill fear and anger in German civilians, urging them to resist.

10

HOLOCAUST

The Holocaust refers to the systematic genocide of European Jews during World War 2. Nazi Germany, along with its collaborators, executed the deliberate murder of approximately six million Jews across the territories under German occupation from 1941 to 1945. This amount accounted for about two-thirds of the Jewish population in Europe. In this chapter, we seek to shed light on crucial facets of this Nazi-driven genocide, including the establishment of concentration and extermination camps, the subsequent liberation of these camps by Allied forces, and an in-depth exploration of different aspects, such as the origins of the term 'Holocaust,' the notion of the 'Final Solution,' the Nazi Plan involving concentration and death camps, gas chambers, systematic persecution and discrimination, as well as the Nuremberg Laws in 1935.

Origin of the Term

The term "holocaust," derived from the Greek words "holos" (whole) and "kaustos" (burned), historically referred to a sacrificial offering consumed by fire on an altar (Garber, 1989). Following their rise to power in Germany in January 1933, the Nazis propagated the belief in the "racial superiority" of Germans. They perceived Jews, labeled as "inferior," as an external menace to the purported German racial community.

The biblical term Shoa, alternatively spelled Sho'ah, translates to "destruction" in the Hebrew language and emerged as the established Hebrew term for the Holocaust by the early 1940s. Many Jews and an increasing number of others prefer the use of Shoah for various reasons, including concerns about the potentially offensive theological connotations associated with the original meaning of the word "holocaust." Some also colloquially refer to the Holocaust as "Auschwitz," transforming this notorious death camp into a symbol representing the entire genocide.

It is noteworthy that the term "genocide" was coined in the context of the Holocaust.

The Nuremberg Laws in 1935

The Nuremberg Laws, instituted in Nazi Germany on September 15, 1935, were deeply rooted in anti-Semitism and racism. This was set in motion during a special session of the Reichstag coinciding with the annual Nuremberg Rally of the Nazi Party. They consisted of two primary laws: the Law for the Protection of German Blood and German Honor, which forbade marriages and relationships between Jews and Germans, and the Reich Citizenship Law, which limited Reich citizenship to those of German or related blood, leaving others as state subjects without citizenship rights. A supplementary decree on November 14 defined the criteria for being considered Jewish, and the Reich Citizenship Law officially took effect on that date. Later, on November 26, 1935, the laws were expanded to include Romani and Black individuals, placing them in the same category as Jews.

Prosecutions under these laws did not begin until after the 1936 Summer Olympics in Berlin and were driven by foreign policy concerns. After Hitler's rise to power in 1933, the Nazis implemented anti-Semitic policies, aiming to create a Volksgemeinschaft (people's community) based on racial criteria. On April 1, 1933, Hitler declared a national boycott of Jewish businesses, and on April 7, the Law for the Restoration of the Professional Civil Service excluded non-Aryans from various professions. Additionally, a nationwide book burning on May 10 targeted books deemed un-German, including those by Jewish authors. Jewish citizens faced harassment, attacks, and systematic suppression, leading to the revocation of their citizenship and civil rights, ultimately resulting in their expulsion from German society.

The Nuremberg Laws had severe economic and social consequences for the Jewish community. Those violating the marriage laws were imprisoned, and post-March 8, 1938, they were rearrested by the Gestapo after serving their sentences and sent to Nazi concentration camps. Non-Jews gradually avoided socializing with Jews, leading to the closure of Jewish-owned stores. With Jews barred from certain professions, middle-class business owners and professionals were forced into menial jobs. Emigration became increasingly challenging, with Jews required to relinquish up to 90% of their wealth as a departure tax. By 1938, finding a country willing to accept potential Jewish emigrants became nearly impossible. The Nazis' mass deportation plans, such as the Madagascar Plan, proved unworkable, prompting the initiation of the mass extermination of European Jews in mid-1941.

"The Final Solution"

The Final Solution, also called the Final Solution to the Jewish Question, was the systematic Nazi plan to eliminate individuals identified as Jews during World War 2. Serving as the official code name for the comprehensive murder of Jews, the Final Solution extended beyond the borders of the European continent. This calculated and methodical genocide unfolded across the entire German-occupied Europe, reaching its tragic culmination during the Holocaust and resulting in the death of 90% of the Polish Jews and two-thirds of the whole of the European Jewish population. It is important to note that the Final Solution did not encompass the hundreds of thousands of Jews killed by Romanian forces before World War 2, representing a significant operational deviation from the Nazi Final Solution.

The origins and progression of decisions leading to the Final Solution are subjects of intense study and debate within the context of the Holocaust. This program evolved over the initial 25 months of the war, climaxing in the objective to "murder every last Jew in the German grasp." Holocaust historian Christopher Browning underscores that the Final Solution cannot be attributed to a single decision at a specific moment but rather evolved through a protracted and gradual decision-making process.

In 1940, after the Fall of France, Adolf Eichmann proposed the Madagascar Plan to relocate Europe's Jewish population to the French colony. However, logistical challenges, particularly a naval blockade, led to the abandonment of this plan. Initial considerations also included deporting Jews to Palestine and Siberia. As written by Raul Hilberg in 1941, the mass murder unfolded in two phases: the mobile killing units that pursued victims across occupied eastern territories, succeeded by the transportation of Jewish victims on death trains to centralized extermination camps across German-occupied Europe.

The Nazi invasion of the Soviet Union under Operation Barbarossa in June 1941 triggered a "war of annihilation," opening doors to the systematic mass murder of European Jews. For Hitler, Bolshevism symbolized the "most recent and most nefarious manifestation of the eternal Jewish threat." Wehrmacht Joint Operations Staff Chief

Alfred Jodl reiterated Hitler's stance, emphasizing the need to eliminate the "Jewish-Bolshevik intelligentsia." In May 1941, Gestapo leader Heinrich Müller acknowledged the perceived danger from the civilian population and justified limiting the jurisdiction of military courts in prosecuting troops.

By the end of December 1941 and before the Wannsee Conference, more than 439,800 Jewish people had perished, and the Final Solution policy in the East became widely known within the SS. Reports indicated entire regions as "free of Jews" by the Einsatzgruppen. While addressing district governors in the General Government, Governor-General Hans Frank hinted at the impracticality of settling Jews in Ostland and the Reichskommissariat and suggested self-liquidation. In this context, Heinrich Himmler's discussion with Hitler resulted in the directive to "exterminate them as partisans." According to Yehuda Bauer, this remark is as close as historians might get to a definitive order from Hitler for the Holocaust's genocide. Within two years, the total number of shooting victims in the East rose to between 618,000 and 800,000 Jews.

Concentration Camps

From 1933 to 1945, Nazi Germany operated a network of over a thousand concentration camps, which included sub-camps on its home turf and in various parts of German-occupied Europe. Initially directed at political opponents like Communists or Social Democrats, the first official concentration camp, located in Dachau (near Munich), opened its doors in March 1933 with an initial focus on detaining the Communists.

As World War 2 unfolded, the scope of persecution broadened to encompass other minority groups, with Jews becoming the primary target. However, by the war's conclusion, numerous other groups, including Roma, homosexuals, and anti-Nazi civilians from occupied territories, had also faced liquidation. With the onset of the war, camp inmates became an additional labor force, leading to the proliferation of such camps across Europe. Inmates were coerced into working for their sustenance; those unable to work often succumbed to starvation, while those enduring the harsh conditions often perished from overwork. The most egregious manifestation of this system was the establishment of extermination centers, or "death camps," primarily situated in Poland, where Adolf Hitler conceived his "final solution" to the "Jewish problem." Auschwitz, Majdanek, and Treblinka emerged as the most notorious examples. Certain camps, like Buchenwald, served as venues for medical experimentation involving the testing of toxins, antitoxins, surgical techniques, and artificially induced diseases on living human subjects.

The first camps were opened in March 1933, shortly after Adolf Hitler assumed the Chancellorship of Germany. After the 1934 purge of the SA, the SS, through the Concentration Camps Inspectorate and later the SS Main Economic and Administrative Office, assumed exclusive administration of the concentration camps. Initially dominated by members of the Communist Party of Germany, the inmate population diversified over time to include different groups like "habitual criminals," "asocials," and Jews. As World War 2 progressed, individuals from German-occupied Europe were incarcerated in these camps. Approximately 1.65 million individuals were registered prisoners, with about a million perishing during imprisonment. The majority of fatalities occurred in the latter half of World War 2, with at least a third of the 700,000 registered prisoners as of January 1945 losing their lives. Following Allied military victories, the gradual liberation of the camps took place in 1944 and 1945, although hundreds of thousands of prisoners succumbed during the death marches.

Gas Chambers and Crematoria

The gas chambers serve as a chilling testament to the horrors of the Holocaust, embodying Nazi Germany's utilization of various methods for mass murder during this tragic period.

From 1939, gas chambers were initially employed as part of the Aktion T4, an "involuntary euthanasia" initiative. Here the Nazis systematically exterminated individuals with physical and intellectual disabilities, deeming them "unworthy of life." The initial experiments in gassing patients occurred in October 1939 in occupied Posen, Poland, resulting in the carbon monoxide poisoning of hundreds of prisoners in an improvised gas chamber. By 1940, gas chambers utilizing bottled pure carbon monoxide were operational at at least six killing centers in Germany. Beyond targeting those with disabilities, these centers were also used during Action 14f13 to eliminate prisoners moved from concentration camps in Germany, Austria, and Poland. Strikingly, the murder of concentration camp inmates persisted even after the official cessation of the euthanasia program in 1941.

During the invasion of Russia, Einsatzgruppen conducted mass executions using gas vans—trucks modified to direct engine exhaust into a sealed interior gas chamber. From 1941 onward, gas chambers played a significant role in the extermination camps in Poland, where Jews, Roma, and other Holocaust victims were systematically murdered. Gas vans were employed at the Chełmno extermination camp, while the Operation Reinhard camps at Bełżec, Sobibór, and Treblinka utilized exhaust fumes from stationary diesel engines. In a quest for more efficient killing methods, the Nazis experimented with Zyklon-B, a hydrogen cyanide-based fumigant, at the Auschwitz concentration camp. This method was subsequently adopted for mass murder at Auschwitz and Majdanek, where up to 6,000 victims were gassed with Zyklon-B each day.

Most gas chambers at extermination camps were either dismantled or destroyed in the final months of World War 2 as Soviet troops advanced, except for those at Dachau, Sachsenhausen, and Majdanek. Notably, one reconstructed gas chamber at Auschwitz stands out as a haunting memorial to the atrocities committed during this dark chapter in history.

11

HOME FRONTS

T he Second World War claimed millions of lives and rendered
countless individuals homeless. This conflict had far-reaching
consequences, which we seek to explore in this chapter. Some of the
key themes discussed in this chapter include the profound effects
of war on civilians, especially children, encompassing physical, financial, and psychological dimensions. Additionally, we will delve
into the themes of displacement and the plight of refugees, along
with the widespread destruction of infrastructure in regions directly
affected by the war.

Rationing

As a result of the war, there were widespread shortages, particularly
in essential commodities such as food and fuel. These challenges
persisted even after the declaration of peace, as war-torn Europe and
Japan struggled to meet the demands for domestic consumption,
let alone exports. In response, nations involved in the conflict, such
as the United Kingdom and the United States, implemented food
rationing programs.

The United Kingdom initiated rationing in January 1940, with the
Ministry of Food overseeing the equitable distribution of limited resources during a time of national scarcity. Every individual,
including women and children, received a ration book containing

coupons necessary for acquiring restricted goods. This points-based system covered items like milk, eggs, tinned goods, dried fruit, cereals, and biscuits.

Similarly, the United States enforced rationing on essential supplies, including food, shoes, metal, paper, and rubber. Individuals, including infants, were allocated a specific number of "points" that, along with money, were required to purchase restricted items. As an example, in 1943, a pound of bacon cost around 30 cents, but buyers had to surrender seven ration points along with the payment. These points were distributed to citizens as stamps in booklets during the war. The Office of Price Administration (OPA) managed the rationing program, relying extensively on volunteers to distribute ration books and explain the system to the users and merchants. By the end of the war, approximately 5,600 local rationing boards, staffed by over 100,000 citizen volunteers, were administering the program. Priority allocations, such as milk and eggs for women and children, were granted to those in dire need.

As shortages intensified, long queues became common, with individuals often discovering that the desired items had run out when reaching the front.

Impact of Propaganda

During the Second World War, the British government recognized the significant role of boosting morale on the Home Front in supporting the armed services deployed overseas. As individuals on the Home Front actively contributed to the production of military equipment, maintaining their morale and confidence in the ultimate victory became increasingly crucial.

In this context, propaganda played a significant role in shaping attitudes on both sides of the conflict during the Second World

War. In 1942, the Office of War Information (OWI) was established in the United States to spearhead the propaganda initiative, scripting and disseminating government messages. A creative assembly of artists, filmmakers, and intellectuals formed a dynamic "factory floor," producing posters, pamphlets, newsreels, radio shows, and movies—all crafted to ensure unwavering public support for the war efforts.

Posters were a prominent component of the OWI's output and were mass-produced and distributed nationwide. They adorned diverse locations, including train stations, post offices, schools, churches, factories, and grocery stores. Serving a dual purpose, the posters aimed to encourage and inspire Americans while also conveying warnings, rebukes, and alarms. Psychological tactics, guilt, and emotional appeals were employed to tap into patriotism and loyalty. Addressing concerns such as safety, posters urged Americans to wear white while walking during blackouts so that they were not hit by a car (s) and emphasized caution at work to prevent injuries that could potentially hamper production and strain hospital resources.

Characters like "Axidunce" and "Benny the Bungler" were introduced to symbolize carelessness that assisted Axis foes by causing accidents. Posters actively promoted responsible and healthy living, emphasizing the impact of vices on production. Simultaneously, Americans were encouraged to minimize the wastage of essential resources such as food, clothing, rubber, water, and fuel. They were instructed to grow their own food through subsistence farming, engage in canning and preservation, and stretch their rations—all in support of the soldiers. Contributions to the war funds through the purchase of bonds were also emphasized as a patriotic duty.

Impact on Civilians

The total estimate of casualties in the Second World War varies due to numerous unrecorded deaths. It is widely suggested that around 70-85 million people lost their lives during the conflict, comprising approximately 20 million military personnel and 50 million civilians. The civilian casualties resulted from deliberate acts of genocide, massacres, mass bombings, diseases, and starvation.

The Soviet Union, enduring staggering losses, witnessed approximately 27 million casualties, with 8.7 million military and 19 million civilian deaths. Among military casualties, roughly 5.7 million were ethnic Russians, followed by 1.3 million ethnic Ukrainians. Germany faced significant military losses, totaling 5.3 million, primarily on the Eastern Front and during the war's final battles. Out of overall deaths in World War 2, approximately 85 percent, mainly Soviet and Chinese, occurred on the Allied side, while 15 percent were on the Axis side. War crimes committed by German and Japanese troops in occupied territories resulted in a significant number of deaths, including the systematic genocide of 6 million Jews throughout the Holocaust and an additional 5 to 6 million from various ethnic and minority groups.

In the Asia-Pacific region, between 3 million and over 10 million civilians, predominantly Chinese, were killed by Japanese occupation forces. Moreover, devastating atrocities, such as the Nanking Massacre, claimed the lives of hundreds of thousands of Chinese civilians. Both Axis and Allied forces employed biological and chemical weapons, testing them on civilians and prisoners of war. The Soviet Union was responsible for the Katyn massacre and the imprisonment or execution of political prisoners. Mass bombings targeted civilian areas, constituting potential war crimes. The German Luftwaffe targeted hospitals and fleeing refugees, while the

Western Allies bombed cities like Tokyo, Dresden, Hamburg, and Cologne. These bombings resulted in the destruction of over 160 cities and the death of over 600,000 German civilians.

Moreover, as we have discussed in our previous chapter, the Nazi government, led by Adolf Hitler, orchestrated the Holocaust, resulting in the deliberate extermination of approximately 6 million Jews deemed "unworthy of life." Around 12 million forced laborers, primarily Eastern Europeans, were employed in the German war economy.

Additionally, Soviet gulags (a government agency in charge of the Soviet network of forced labor camps set up by Lenin) contributed to the deaths of citizens from occupied countries and German prisoners of war. Suspicion of Nazi collaboration led to the mistreatment of Soviet ex-Prisoners of War and the repatriated civilians, with some sent to the Gulag after scrutiny by the NKVD (Russian acronym for People's Commissariat of Internal Affairs).

Role of Minorities

During the Second World War, white Americans constituted the majority of the U.S. Army, with minority groups including African Americans, Native Americans, Jewish Americans, Chinese Americans, and Hispanics, amongst others. All ethnic groups, encompassing both the majority whites and ethnic minorities, expressed unwavering determination to enlist in the U.S. Army following the Japanese attack on Pearl Harbor on December 7, 1941. Despite encountering mistreatment and discrimination, they valiantly served and defended the country.

Until the later stages of the war in 1945, the total number of African American soldiers in the armed forces reached 1,056,841, comprising approximately 11% of all American soldiers. While serving in the military, these soldiers also ardently fought for their civil rights, facing unequal treatment due to the Jim Crow laws, a system of racial segregation imposed by the military. These laws mandated separate accommodations, medical facilities, and work assignments for African American soldiers, highlighting the racial disparities they endured.

Despite the challenges, World War 2 presented economic and psychological opportunities for American minorities and women of all races. The escalating demand for defense industries and President Roosevelt's initiative to create high-skilled, well-paying jobs for previously excluded individuals boosted morale and overall prospects for minorities in the US. This economic empowerment contributed to increased self-confidence and a sense of belonging.

Impact on Children

The Second World War had profound effects on children worldwide, with many facing separation from families, the destruction of homes, and the tragic loss of parents. A significant challenge confronted by children was evacuation, as millions in Britain were sent to safer locations due to the government's voluntary evacuation scheme, driven by the fear of German bombings. Families opting to send their loved ones overseas added to this exodus.

Besides, the war significantly disrupted children's education, with one in five schools damaged by bombing and others requisitioned by the government. Large classrooms, limited supplies of stationery and books, and the departure of young male teachers to join the forces marked this period. Once the war was over, a substantial number of children struggled to attain the required levels of literacy and numeracy.

Children of varying ages in the United Kingdom contributed to the war effort in different capacities. Older boys and girls often joined the Boy Scouts and Girl Guides, supporting Air Raid Precautions as messengers or fire-watchers. Younger children played roles in collecting war materials, fundraising for munitions, and knitting comforts for troops. The war's impact on children's health manifested in various ways, including common issues like head lice, skin diseases, and malnutrition due to the rationing of essential items. However, the most significant toll was on their mental health, with ten percent of the country's population evacuated, mainly children, requiring support to cope with separation and the loss of homes and family members. Childhood itself underwent transformations, marked by a scarcity of new toys and clothes, as children actively participated in the war effort through salvage collection, running errands, and assisting with farming.

Displacement and Refugees

As we have highlighted earlier, the war had a profound impact on millions of people, particularly in Europe, where approximately 65 million individuals faced displacement. This diverse group included those subjected to Nazi slave labor, former Prisoners of War, and countless others whose homes had been bombed and shelled. The United Nations Relief and Rehabilitation Administration (UNRRA) was established in 1943 to address the burning needs of these individuals. It was tasked with planning, coordinating, and administering relief measures, which encompassed food, fuel, clothing, shelter, medical services, and other essentials for war victims in areas under the control of the United Nations.

Post–World War 2, Europe witnessed the creation of displaced persons camps in Germany, Austria, and Italy, specifically for refugees from Eastern Europe and former inmates of Nazi concentration camps. By the time the war ended, a staggering 40 million people had been displaced from their home countries, with approximately 11 million seeking refuge in Allied-occupied Germany. This diverse population included released prisoners of war, liberated slave laborers, and survivors of both non-Jewish and Jewish concentration camps. These displaced individuals were collectively referred to as "displaced persons" (DPs), and the United Nations Relief and Rehabilitation Administration (UNRRA) assumed responsibility for their care.

Between 1945 and 1952, over 250,000 Jewish displaced persons (DPs) resided in camps and urban centers in Germany, Austria, and Italy. The impact of the war in Asia mirrored the displacement challenges seen in Europe. The conflict, coupled with the swift postwar decolonization of the region, led to the displacement of millions. The imperial formation that characterized Northeast Asia from the 1890s to 1945, involving the Japanese Empire in conflict with the Qing Empire and later the Republic of China, underwent a significant transformation. Japan's expansionist policies, culminating in war with China and the United States, ultimately led to its surrender in 1945, resulting in the loss of both the war and the empire.

Collaboration and Resistance

Collaboration, irrespective of its varied forms and motivations, consistently implied support for Nazi Germany, particularly in the management of the war. In 1968, Historian Stanley Hoffmann introduced a distinction between the first form—"state collaboration," driven by necessity, either voluntary or involuntary, aiming to maintain public order and economic stability—and the second form, intentional and individual, known as "collaborationism." Polish historian Czesław Madajczyk further differentiated between "harmful" and "useful" collaboration. Yet, the boundaries between these categories often blurred, as some ultra-collaborationists viewed their actions as patriotic.

Whether through occupations or alliances, collaboration was grounded in shared interests. Nazi Germany relied on occupied countries, satellite states, and allies for supply and provisioning, making their cooperation indispensable for the war effort. By adhering to Nazi positions, collaborating governments legitimized aggressive policies and persecution. In return, collaborating countries sought a more honorable position in the new European order under German domination, aiming to protect their independence or revise post-1918 peace treaties. This trend was evident as early as 1938 when Balkan states sought protection from the USSR's expansionist designs. In 1940, Vichy France aimed to safeguard territorial integrity while exploiting the defeat to establish a totalitarian regime.

Berlin deployed official and unofficial agents abroad to encourage collaboration, emphasizing anti-Communist and anti-Semitic currents and presenting the German regime as a model of modernity. Notable figures in this effort included Otto Abetz, the ambassador in occupied Paris from 1940 to 1944, and Rudolf Rahn, Manfred von Killinger, Edmund Veesenmayer, and Hermann Neubacher, who managed the economies of South Eastern Europe. Economic, military, and security considerations took precedence over ideological questions. Berlin prioritized collaboration from traditional elites willing to cooperate and maintain order and showed little inclination to embrace extremist collaborators.

On the other hand, the invasion of the USSR in 1941 marked a turning point, intensifying collaboration across Europe. The Reich stepped up with its demands on its partners for weapons, food, workers, and combatants. Simultaneously, resistance movements emerged in occupied countries despite severe repression. Initially

willing to collaborate, the elites in power gradually withdrew support.

12
END OF THE WAR

O n April 30, 1945, Germany, left with no alternative, surrendered to the Allied forces. Subsequently, control over
Germany was divided amongst four nations: the United States,
France, the United Kingdom, and the Soviet Union. Western Berlin
fell under the administration of the Western countries – the United
Kingdom, the United States, and France – while the Soviet Union
administered East Berlin. Hitler and his wife chose joint suicide,
marking the culmination of events six years after Germany's invasion of Poland on September 1, 1939.

The physical toll of the Second World War was massive, as it
claimed an estimated 70-85 million lives, roughly 3% of the world's
population at the time. Amongst these victims were Jews, who
were systematically persecuted and killed in German concentration
camps during the Holocaust. Approximately a month after the
United States dropped atomic bombs on Hiroshima and Nagasaki
on August 6, which resulted in the deaths of about 110,000 people
(70,000 in Hiroshima and 40,000 in Nagasaki), the war officially
ended on September 2, 1945.

In this book's final chapter, we seek to shed light on the events
of the war's concluding months. Key occurrences include Operation Thunderclap, the Battle of Okinawa, the Soviet Invasion of
Manchuria, and the Yalta Conference. Additionally, we will explore
the establishment of significant global organizations such as the

United Nations, the emergence of a new international economic system, and the decolonization of Asia and Africa. Several nations, including India, Pakistan, Indonesia, the Philippines, and various Arab countries, were granted independence during this transformative period.

The Allied Bombing Campaigns and Final Battles

The total surrender of Nazi Germany to the Allied forces was marked by a pact formalized by Field Marshal Wilhelm Keitel on May 8, 1945, in Karlshorst, Berlin. After this date, some battles were still being fought in European theater during World War 2. Following Adolf Hitler's suicide and Grand Admiral Karl Dönitz taking over power in May 1945, Soviet forces seized control of Berlin and accepted the surrender of the Dönitz-led government. The final clashes occurred on the Eastern Front, culminating in the comprehensive surrender of all the remaining German armed forces. Notable instances include the surrender of Army Group Courland in the Baltics on May 10, 1945, and the Prague offensive in Czechoslovakia on May 11, 1945.

In April 1945, the Western Allies took 1,500,000 prisoners on the Western Front, with an additional 120,000 German troops captured in the closing Italian campaign. Over the preceding three to four months, more than 800,000 German soldiers surrendered on the Eastern Front. The establishment of the Rheinwiesenlager camps in western Germany began in early April, governed by the Allies to detain Axis Forces personnel. Notably, the Supreme Headquarters Allied Expeditionary Force (SHAEF) reclassified prisoners as Disarmed Enemy Forces, sidestepping Geneva Convention provisions.

By October, thousands had perished in the camps due to starvation, exposure, and disease.

The liberation of Germany exposed the enormity of the Holocaust, corroborating the findings of Pilecki's 1943 Report. Allied forces uncovered Nazi concentration camps and forced labor facilities during their advance. Bergen-Belsen, liberated on April 15, 1945, housed up to 60,000 prisoners. Dachau was discovered four days later by the American 42nd Infantry Division. Allied troops compelled the remaining SS guards to bury the corpses in mass graves. The revelation of these atrocities led to the trial and sentencing of the captured SS guards at war crime tribunals.

On April 25, 1945, the last German troops retreated from Finnish Lapland into occupied Norway. Simultaneously, Italian partisans liberated Milan and Turin. On April 27, Italian dictator Benito Mussolini was captured, and on April 28, he was executed. On April 29, Rodolfo Graziani surrendered all Fascist Italian armed forces. On April 30, Adolf Hitler died by suicide in his Führerbunker, acknowledging the Battle of Nuremberg, the Battle of Hamburg, and the encroaching Battle in Berlin.

On April 29, Oberstleutnant Schweinitz and Sturmbannführer Wenner, representing Generaloberst Heinrich von Vietinghoff and SS Obergruppenführer Karl Wolff, surrendered by signing a surrender document at Caserta. The Germans agreed to a ceasefire and surrender on May 2 at 2 pm. Following intense discussions between Wolff and Albert Kesselring, nearly 1,000,000 men in Austria and Italy surrendered completely to British Field Marshal Sir Harold Alexander.

The Battle of Berlin concluded on May 2, with General der Artillerie Helmuth Weidling surrendering the city to General Vasily Chuikov of the Red Army. On the same day, the commanders of the two armies of Army Group Vistula north of Berlin surrendered to the Western Allies. May 2 is also believed to be the day when Martin Bormann died, as witnessed by Artur Axmann near Lehrter Bahnhof railway station: his cause of death, however, remains unknown. The Potsdam Agreement, signed on August 1, 1945, outlined plans for the postwar German government, territorial boundaries, annexations, and the expulsion of remaining Germans from annexed territories. French representatives on the Allied Control Council, not part of the Potsdam Conference, rejected obligations outlined in the agreement, leaving many aspects unimplemented.

The Fall of Berlin

The Battle of Berlin was designated the Berlin Strategic Offensive Operation by the Soviet Union and is known as the Fall of Berlin. It also stood as one of the final significant offensives in the European theater of World War 2. Unfolding from April 20 to May 2, 1945, it culminated in the Soviet Red Army's capture of Berlin, driven by a determination to avenge the suffering endured by the Soviet people since 1941.

In April 1945, the Soviet Union amassed one of the most substantial concentrations of military power ever witnessed outside Berlin. The city, battered by repeated Allied bombings, found its remaining populace shielded by a makeshift force comprising stragglers and remnants of shattered formations, alongside militia and units of the Hitler Youth—some of whom, with an average age of 14, were thrust into battle.

Soviet marshals Ivan Konev and Georgiy Zhukov engaged in a relentless race to seize the glory of capturing Berlin, displaying a readiness to accept staggering casualties and inflict colossal damage. Within a span of five days, the two forces linked up and encircled Berlin. The final assault witnessed Soviet artillery firing nearly two million shells. Berliners could only seek refuge in their cellars, hoping that rumors of relief or a potential alliance between the Americans and Germany against the Red Army might materialize.

The urban terrain offered some advantages to the defenders, as the hurried Red Army tanks lacked adequate infantry support. The Hitler Youth, displaying remarkable courage, often ambushed Soviet tanks with Panzerfaust antitank rockets. However, the overwhelming firepower of the Soviets, including artillery and Katyusha rockets, countered these efforts. Suspicion of defenders in cellars prompted Soviet grenades, with little regard for civilian lives.

In the heart of the city, Adolf Hitler, ensconced in his bunker, clung to the belief that Berlin could be saved. He issued futile orders to the non-existent armies to break the siege. Meanwhile, despite its strategic insignificance, Joseph Stalin was fixated on capturing the Reichstag building. This obsession incurred a heavy toll on the number of Soviet soldiers lost.

Amid the desperation of Berliners eager for the nightmare to end, some hung white or red flags from their windows, signaling surrender or even welcome to the Red Army. However, this act risked execution by the SS firing squads, and there is little evidence that Soviet troops paid attention. As the Red Army closed in on the final pockets of resistance, Hitler's suicide on April 30 presented General Helmuth Weidling, the garrison commander, with an opportunity to surrender. SS troops faced doom if captured, leading some to fight on while others chose suicide. Relieved that the ordeal was over, the majority emerged to confront the extensive devastation inflicted upon the city of Berlin and come to terms with its new conquerors. The general surrender of German forces concluded five days later, with the Red Army enduring 100,000 casualties and the precise count of German deaths remaining unknown.

Potsdam Conference

The Big Three, Soviet leader Joseph Stalin, British Prime Minister Winston Churchill (later replaced by Prime Minister Clement Attlee on July 26), and U.S. President Harry Truman, convened in Potsdam, Germany, between July 17 and August 2, 1945, to negotiate the terms for concluding World War 2. Following the Yalta Conference in February 1945, where Stalin, Churchill, and Roosevelt had agreed to meet post-German surrender to determine postwar European borders, the Allied leaders gathered at Potsdam to continue these discussions. Despite the Allies' commitment to a joint war effort in the Pacific, the absence of a common European enemy posed challenges in reaching a consensus on postwar reconstruction.

The central issue at Potsdam revolved around how to handle Germany. At Yalta, the Soviets had advocated for substantial postwar reparations from Germany, with half allocated to the Soviet Union. While Roosevelt had agreed to these demands, Truman and Secretary of State James Byrnes sought to temper Germany's treatment by allowing occupying nations to extract reparations solely from their respective zones. Truman and Byrnes endorsed this stance to avoid a recurrence of the situation spawned by the Treaty of Versailles, which had imposed hefty reparations on Germany after World War 1, hindering its economy and also contributing to the rise of the Nazis.

However, despite numerous disagreements, the Allied leaders did reach certain agreements at Potsdam. They confirmed the status of a demilitarized and disarmed Germany under four Allied occupation zones. The Protocol of the Conference outlined complete disarmament and demilitarization, dismantling German industry with military potential, eliminating military and paramilitary forces, and a ban on the production of military hardware in Germany. Additionally, German society was slated for democratic restructuring through the repeal of Nazi-era discriminatory laws, the arrest and trial of deemed "war criminals," and the purge of authoritarian influences from the educational and judicial systems. Democratic political parties were encouraged to participate at local and state levels. However, the reconstitution of a national German government was deferred indefinitely, with the Allied Control Commission overseeing the country during this interim period.

A contentious matter at Potsdam involved revising German-Soviet-Polish borders and expelling several million Germans from disputed territories. Poland received a substantial portion of German territory in exchange for land lost to the Soviet Union, initiating the deportation of German residents. While the British and Americans feared a mass exodus destabilizing Western occupation zones, they took no action beyond declaring that any transfers should occur orderly and humanely, urging a temporary suspension of deportations by Poland, Czechoslovakia, and Hungary.

Beyond Germany and Poland, the Potsdam negotiators authorized the establishment of a Council of Foreign Ministers tasked with drafting peace treaties for Germany's former allies. They also agreed to revise the 1936 Montreux Convention, granting Turkey sole control over the Turkish Straits. Additionally, the United States, Great Britain, and China jointly issued the "Potsdam Declaration," threatening Japan with "prompt and utter destruction" unless an immediate surrender occurred (the Soviet Union abstained from signing as it had yet to declare war on Japan).

The Surrender of Japan

The announcement of the surrender of the Japanese Empire in World War 2 came from Emperor Hirohito on August 15. It was formally signed on September 2, 1945, marking the cessation of hostilities. By the end of July 1945, the Imperial Japanese Navy (IJN) had lost its capacity for significant operations, and an Allied invasion of Japan loomed. In the Potsdam Declaration issued on July 26, 1945, the United States, in conjunction with the United Kingdom and China, called for the unconditional surrender of the Japanese armed forces, warning of "prompt and utter destruction" as the only alternative.

Despite publicly expressing their determination to fight until the bitter end, Japan's leaders, known as the "Big Six" or the Supreme Council for the Direction of the War, were secretly reaching out to the ostensibly neutral Soviet Union to explore the possibilities for a peace settlement that would be more favorable to Japan. Simultaneously maintaining diplomatic engagement with Japan to create an impression of potential mediation, the Soviets were covertly preparing for military action against Japanese forces in Manchuria and Korea, extending to South Sakhalin and the Kuril Islands. These actions aligned with undisclosed agreements between the Soviets, the United States, and the United Kingdom during the Tehran and Yalta Conferences.

CONCLUSION

"War does not determine who is right, only who is left." - Bertrand Russell

O verall, the Second World War left a lasting mark on history in various ways. Beyond the extensive loss of lives, the economic costs were also immense. The economic consequences were evident through infrastructure damage, a declining working population, inflation, shortages, uncertainty, and disruption to regular economic activities. Europe, Asia, and Africa lay in ruins, with towns and cities flattened, railroads destroyed, and the countryside scorched. On the one hand, while the American Marshall Plan played an essential role in the rebuilding of Western Europe and Asia, on the other, the war aftermath saw a dichotomy in Europe's spheres of influence, with Western countries and the United States dominating the Western sphere, and the Soviet Union holding sway over Eastern European nations. The war conclusively established the emergence of two global superpowers: the United States and the Soviet Union.

However, despite the harmful effects of the war, certain positive outcomes emerged. Women and minorities worldwide, particularly in the United States, found employment and economic opportunities. Women became an integral part of the workforce even after the return of men from the battlefields. Moreover, the war reshaped the global political landscape, beginning a period of rapid decolonization. Imperial powers, including the British, Dutch, and Belgian Empires, witnessed a swift decline, marked by a shift in focus and a withdrawal from their colonies. This transition significantly impacted the political positions of imperial powers, leading to changes in alliances and geopolitical strategies.

For Germany, a remarkable "economic miracle" unfolded, transforming the post-war landscape of Western Germany into a thriving industrial economy, ultimately becoming the powerhouse of Western Europe. The nation witnessed remarkable growth despite initial skepticism about the economic success of the newly formed German Republics in 1949. Another significant milestone was the establishment of a new international order characterized by the formation of the United Nations after the war. The United Nations Security Council (UNSC) comprised the United States, the United Kingdom, the Soviet Union, France, and China, aiming to foster international cooperation and prevent conflicts.

Simultaneously, the Bretton Woods Conference in July 1944 gave rise to a new economic framework for the post-World War 2 world. Financial organizations such as the International Monetary Fund (IMF) and the International Bank for Reconstruction and Development (IRBD), later part of the World Bank Group, emerged from this agreement, shaping the global economic landscape for three decades until 1973. However, the lasting horrifying impact of the war is evident in the haunting legacy of Hiroshima and Nagasaki, which serve as a collective nightmare for the world to this day.

In conclusion, our intention in this book was to provide readers with a comprehensive exploration of various issues and themes related to the war rather than its aftermath. These themes encompassed different aspects, such as the battles fought, the leaders of both Axis and Allied powers, and the military techniques employed. While by no means an exhaustive encyclopedia on the war, our primary goal within the book's limited space was to furnish readers with as much information and facts as possible, offering a nuanced perspective on the war's diverse facets.

Thank you for reading!

If you enjoyed this book, feel free to leave a review on Amazon. This will help us continue to provide great books and help our potential customers make confident buying decisions. We will be forever grateful - thank you in advance!

REFERENCES

Sennett, A. (2014). Film Propaganda: Triumph of the Will as a Case Study. Framework: The Journal of Cinema and Media, 55(1), 45. https://doi.org/10.13110/framework.55.1.0045

Barbier, M. K. (1998). D-Day Deception: Operation Fortitude and the Normandy invasion. The University of Southern Mississippi.

Barrowclough, D. (2017). Digging for Hitler: The Nazi archaeologists search for an Aryan past. Fonthill Media.

Browning, C. R. (2003). Initiating the Final Solution: The Fateful Months of September–October 1941. United States Holocaust Museum. https://www.ushmm.org/m/pdfs/Publication_OP_1996-01.pdf

Bryant, G. CM (2016). The Women's Army Corps: An assertion of public and private rights. University of Nebraska at Kearney.

Eloranta, J. (2010). Why Did the League of Nations fail? Cliometrica, 5(1), 27–52. https://doi.org/10.1007/s11698-010-0049-9

Stibbe, M. Negotiating and Mediating Conduct of War. International Encyclopedia of the First World War (WW1). (n.d.). Encyclopedia.1914-1918-Online.net . https://encyclopedia.1914-1918-online.net/article/negotiating_and_mediating_conduct_of_war Accessed December 15, 2023.

Garber, Z., & Zuckerman, B. (1989). Why Do We Call the Holocaust "The Holocaust?" An Inquiry into the Psychology of Labels. Modern Judaism, 9(2), 197–211. http://www.jstor.org/stable/1396314

German, K. M. (1990). Frank Capra's Why We Fight series and the American audience. Western Journal of Speech Communication, 54(2), 237–248. https://doi.org/10.1080/10570319009374338

Hughes, R. G. (2020). Carl von Clausewitz and his Philosophy of War: The Evolution of a Reputation, 1831–2021. History, 105(368), 773–805. https://doi.org/10.1111/1468-229x.13085

Gooderson, I. (1992). Heavy and medium bombers: How successful were they in the tactical close air support role during World War II? Journal of Strategic Studies, 15(3), 367–399. https://doi.org/10.1080/01402399208437490

Hung, C.-T. (2020). War and Popular Culture: resistance in modern China, 1937-1945. Univ of California Press.

Cory, J. M. (1943). Libraries and the Office of War Information. ALA Bulletin, 37(2), 38–41. https://www.jstor.org/stable/pdf/25691596.pdf

Marks, S. (2013). Mistakes and Myths: The Allies, Germany, and the Versailles Treaty, 1918–1921. The Journal of Modern History, 85(3), 632–659.

Moser, J. E. (2015). Global Great Depression and the Coming of World War II. Routledge.

Museen. (n.d.). History of "Racism and anti-Semitism" | Documentation Center Nazi Party Rally Grounds. Museums.nuernberg.de. Retrieved February 17, 2024, from https://museums.nuernberg.de/documentation-center/topics/national-socialism/racism-and-anti-semitism/racism-and-anti-semitism Accessed December 15, 2023.

United States Holocaust Memorial Museum. (2019, September 11). Nuremberg Laws. Ushmm.org; United States Holocaust Memorial Museum. https://encyclopedia.ushmm.org/content/en/article/nuremberg-laws Accessed December 15, 2023.

First World War.com - Feature Articles - Of Fraud and Force Fast Woven: Domestic Propaganda During The First World War.

(n.d.). Www.firstworldwar.com. https://www.firstworldwar.co m/features/propaganda.htm

Osborne, B., & Army War Coll Carlisle PA (1990). Propaganda tool: the Hollywood war movie and its usurpation by TV. US Army War College.

Paksoy, T. (2017). Cradle of Triumph: The Invasion of Sicily and the Anglo-American Alliance in the Second World War [PhD diss. Cradle of Triumph: The Invasion of Sicily and the Anglo-American Alliance in the Second World War], Bilkent Universitesi (Turkey).

Metcalf, M. (n.d.). Research Guides: Rosie the Riveter: Working Women and World War II: Office of War Information. Guides.loc.gov. https://guides.loc.gov/rosie-the-riveter/office-of-war -information Accessed December 15, 2023.

Roosevelt, F. D. (1988). On War Against Japan: Franklin D. Roosevelt's " Day of Infamy" Address of 1941. National Archives and Records Administratio.

Smith, M. G. (2021). The Influence of Anti-Semitic Imagery and Rhetoric in Germany During the Early to Mid-20th Century [PhD diss. The Influence of Anti-Semitic Imagery and Rhetoric in Germany During the Early to Mid-20th Century]. Monterey, CA; Naval Postgraduate School.

Sitter, M. (2013). Violence and masculinity in Hollywood war films during World War II [PhD diss. Violence and masculinity in Hollywood war films during World War II].

Tavares, E. (2012). Operation fortitude: The closed loop d-day deception plan [Biblioscholar Dissertations Operation fortitude: The closed loop d-day deception plan].

National Geographic. (2022, May 20). Jun 28, 1919 CE: Treaty of Versailles | National Geographic Society. Education.nationalgeographic.org; National Geographic. https://education.natio nalgeographic.org/resource/treaty-versailles-ends-wwi/ Accessed December 11, 2023.

Vashem, Y. (1940, July 3). The Nazis & the Jews: The Madagascar Plan. Www.jewishvirtuallibrary.org. https://www.jewishvirtual library.org/the-madagascar-plan-2

Von Clausewitz, C., & Gatzke, H. W. (2003). Principles of war. Courier Corporation.

Walker, M. (2023). A Journal of Film Criticism II [Film].Michael Walker Melodrama and the American Cinema. 2-38.

Welch, D. (2004). Nazi Propaganda and the Volksgemeinschaft: Constructing a People's Community. Journal of Contemporary History, 39(2), 213–238. https://www.jstor.org/stable/3180722

StackPath. (n.d.). World War II Posters. Oklahoma State University Library. Library.okstate.edu . https://library.okstate.edu/search-and-find/collections/digital -collections/world-war-ii-posters/ Accessed December 15, 2023.

Garber, Z., & Zuckerman, B. (1989). Why Do We Call the Holocaust "The Holocaust?" An Inquiry into the Psychology of Labels. Modern Judaism, 9(2), 197–211. https://www.jstor.org/sta ble/1396314 Accessed December 15, 2023.

Printed in Great Britain
by Amazon